Praise for

GRACE FILLED M.

"Grace is to a marriage what oil is to an engine. It lubricates the machinery. In this much-needed book by a very seasoned expert, Tim Kimmel hands out help. Don't miss out!"

Max Lucado
Pastor and Best-Selling Author

"There are a lot of books written on marriage. I've written some of them. But every once in a while one comes along that blows such fresh new air over the subject that further discussion on marriage has to forever factor in these original and innovative ideas. The Kimmels did this, big time, in *Grace Filled Marriage*. You're gonna LOVE this book!"

Dr. Kevin Leman
Author of *Sheet Music* and *A New Husband by Friday*

"As followers of Christ, we are admonished to 'be completely humble and gentle; be patient, bearing with one another in love' (Eph. 4:2 NIV). That's how we extend grace to one another. And as Tim and Darcy Kimmel note in their excellent book, nowhere is this more important than in the institution of marriage."

Jim Daly
President of Focus on the Family

"'Amazing Grace' is normally sung in church. Tragically, we don't often follow God's example and show such grace to our spouses. Tim Kimmel gives practical ideas on how we can bring great harmony to our marriages by showing grace to each other. I highly recommend *Grace Filled Marriage*."

Gary Chapman, Ph.D.
Author of *The Five Love Languages*

"We love this book! And we love Tim and Darcy Kimmel. They are the real deal when it comes to marriage. If you're looking for an authentic and proven message to strengthen your relationship, look no further. *Grace Filled Marriage* is one of the best marriage messages you'll find. It's a game-changer. Biblically grounded, immeasurably practical, and desperately needed—you don't want to miss this. We'll be recommending this book to couples for years."

Drs. Les & Leslie Parrott
Authors of *The Good Fight* and *Making Happy*

"Tim Kimmel's insights and depth of knowledge on 'family matters' have blessed me and so many people with sound biblical teaching and innovative resources. Tim has a way of igniting fresh understanding using simple illustrations to clarify deep spiritual truths. *Grace Filled Marriage* is no exception. I know we will all be blessed by Tim's teaching on how grace can strengthen good marriages, heal failing marriages, and protect new marriages. The impact of grace in marriage makes this a must read."

Dr. Ed Young
Senior Pastor of Second Baptist Church, Houston, Texas

"Grace and forgiveness are two sides of the same coin that in the spiritual bank account of any marriage makes a couple rich toward God. Your marriage and mine can indeed move 'from good to grace.' My friend Tim Kimmel captures in the title *Grace Filled Marriage* one of the critical components to a lifelong marriage of *agape* love. Grace goes beyond the human concept of fairness to reflect the favor God has shown to us. This book will help you expand the portfolio value of your marriage with the investment of time and obedience to this key biblical principle."

Mark L. Bailey
President of Dallas Theological Seminary

"Tim and Darcy are the real deal. They are wonderfully known in my world for living out the grace of God in their marriage. Tim is able to defuse fears with humor and give hope with truth tried out from every angle. *Grace Filled Marriage* is wonderfully practical hope, displaying what grace looks like when it is freed."

John Lynch
Author of *On My Worst Day* and Coauthor of *The Cure*

"I love it when someone can take years of experience, deep knowledge of the Scriptures, and a winsome way with words and actually offer something no one else is saying (but desperately needs to be said). This book isn't a facelift for your marriage, it's a heart transplant. Kimmel offers the missing ingredient to the love dynamic, sex life, and the rough roads of your marriage—God's grace. *Grace Filled Marriage* is an absolute game-changer. I LOVE this book!"

Josh D. McDowell
Author and Speaker

"This should be required reading for anyone married three years or more. By then we know we need fresh ideas of how to live with grace. We've given copies to our five married children!"

Susan Alexander Yates
Author and Speaker

"Thanks, Tim and Darcy, for *Grace Filled Marriage*! This book is a treasure. You have reminded us and called us back to the vision of marriage reflecting God's character, especially his unconditional love and grace. Regrettably, guilt-ridden performance has replaced this lofty vision. Although it is good to know and apply helpful relational skills in marriage, if they are not baptized in God's grace they become pathways to frustration. The Kimmels show us how to create a grace-filled environment in which marriage will flourish. This is one of the most important, helpful books on marriage I have read in a decade."

Dr. Crawford W. Loritts Jr.
Author, Speaker, Radio Host,
Senior Pastor of Fellowship Bible Church, Roswell, Georgia

"What a refreshing approach to having a godly and loving marriage through understanding the role that grace plays in your relationship. Grace may be the oil that lubricates and transforms your relationship into the marriage you've always wanted. Grace enables couples who 'know the Scriptures' to actually *live them out* day by day. We highly recommend *Grace Filled Marriage* to all couples who want to have a truly Christian marriage."

David and Claudia Arp
Coauthors of *10 Great Dates: Connecting Faith, Love & Marriage*

"In *Grace Filled Marriage* Tim and Darcy Kimmel have courageously opened their personal lives, giving us a transparent and biblical look at how marriage can be so demandingly 'daily' and yet also a daily adventure in God's grace."

Dr. Darryl DelHousaye
President of Phoenix Seminary

Grace
Filled Marriage

The Missing Piece.
The Place To Start.

Grace

Filled Marriage

Dr. Tim Kimmel
with Darcy Kimmel

WORTHY®
PUBLISHING

Library of Congress Control Number: 2013945023

Names and identifying details of some people mentioned in this book have been changed to protect their privacy.

For foreign and subsidiary rights, contact rights@worthypublishing.com

ISBN: 978-1-61795-466-5 (trade paper)

Cover Design: Christopher Tobias, tobiasdesign.com
Cover Photo: © Janis Christie
Interior Typesetting: Susan Browne Design

Printed in the United States of America

To
Kory and Gail Schuknecht
Jamie and Kim Rasmussen
Barry and Mandy Asmus

Marriage is a tapestry.
We're so grateful for the rich color and texture
these three couples have added to ours.

CONTENTS

—

ACKNOWLEDGMENTS

Most readers skip this page. That's too bad. They miss the chance to meet some great people. But it's more than that. They miss the chance to understand the concerted effort that went into creating what they hold in their hands. I hope that what you find waiting for you after this page raises the emotional, spiritual, and commitment status of your marriage to levels you've never known before. If it does, it's because of people like …

Steve and Pollyanna Stephens, who provided the ideal setting for turning this project from a concept to a workable outline, and Steve and Barbara Uhlmann, who provided the cabin in the woods required to turn a blank Word file into a completed manuscript.

Byron Williamson, Jeana Ledbetter, Jennifer Day, and the cutting-edge giants of publishing at Worthy.

Jennifer Stair, whose ability to put luster on a finished manuscript is truly mystifying.

Steve Green, a master at hooking up the right hoses between an author with an idea and a publisher with a delivery system.

And the team at Family Matters who live to see people transformed by the power of God's grace into instruments of restoration and reformation.

PART 1

WHAT'S GRACE GOT TO DO WITH IT?

CHAPTER 1

The Missing Piece in Your Marriage

—

What *does* grace have to do with marriage?

It has status as the prelude to a meal or the theme of that famous hymn. And it obviously receives a lot of focus at church, but you may not have realized the crucial role grace is supposed to play in your marriage. In fact without it, we're in trouble, because most marriages don't struggle from a lack of love; they struggle from a lack of grace.

When we said "I do," we imagined our marriage would be a natu-ral partnership in which we would consistently feel affirmed, respected, and appreciated. But unless you're reading this book on your honeymoon, you've discovered that marriage is more like an obstacle course—and you're starting to get bruises on your resolve from tripping over so many hurtful things.

Have you ever experienced situations like these in your marriage?

- Your spouse lets loose a few careless words spoken in frustra-tion—but all too frequently. You're starting to avoid her, not knowing when her temper will flare.

- Your spouse doesn't appreciate the things you do for him every day. It's especially frustrating because it's a blended family and you've worked hard to love his kids as though they were your own. You tell yourself that you're grateful to serve your family. But deep down, you feel taken advantage of.
- Your mate thinks she's hilarious when she jokes about you in public. Her friends like her witty one-liners too. But you're tired of forcing a smile when her constant put-downs at your expense are anything but funny.
- You have to endure a condescending bossiness—a push-you-around attitude—that your spouse would never try on anyone else. Just once, you'd like him to treat you with the same respect he shows his friends and coworkers.
- Your wife prides herself on being thrifty. You work hard to provide for your family and think you've earned the right to indulge in a few things. But you're tired of having to ask permission to spend your collective, but hard-earned, money.
- You're weary of your spouse working late nights or going out with his buddies, not caring that your homemade dinner—and your romance—is getting cold.

These inconsiderate attitudes and actions have a way of replacing the spark in your marriage with a dull, burning ache. But do they indicate an absence of love? Not necessarily. Couples who do these kinds of things often love each other. These situations—along with most of the things that hurt or disappoint you in marriage—are caused by an absence of grace. Love may get us married, but it's grace—God's grace—that we need to wrap around that love to keep it healthy, fresh, and strong.

Full Disclosure

Grace is desiring the best for your spouse, even when they may not deserve it. I know, because I married an angel. She married an idiot.

When we drove away from our wedding reception, Darcy didn't realize she was riding next to a man who likes to go down dead-end roads just to make sure they truly lead nowhere. She was holding the hand of a man whose dreams consistently eclipsed his abilities to make those dreams come true. While we're checking off the full-disclosure box, I need to let you know she also married a man who struggled with seeing the little things of life—like his car keys, wallet, and wristwatch. If this wasn't enough, Darcy married me not realizing she'd be slipping into bed each night with a testosterone-filled man who thought she was the most beautiful girl he'd ever met.

Then there was the fact that she didn't know I . . .

- had an aversion to anything on my dinner plate that wasn't meat and potatoes,
- didn't have a working relationship with clothes hangers, and
- was suspicious of anyone who found women's romance novels anywhere close to realistic.

I was a ready-shoot-aim type of guy who thought he had a good track record of making lucky shots. To me, elaborate plans were for posers. I prided myself as a party waiting to happen, which is fine when you're hanging out with friends on Saturday night but very annoying when you're trying to make a living while raising kids.

Fortunately, Darcy and I had a kernel of something that would eventually grow into the defining feature of how we process our life together. It wasn't something that emanated from our personalities, our upbringings, or from some abilities we brought to the arrangement. Its presence in our marriage was in spite of us. In fact, it was our realization that we had gotten to the end of our own abilities that helped us see that our marriage didn't have a chance without it.

We had *grace*.

It was a grace that grew from a faith decision we had both made a couple of years before we decided to cast our marital lot with each other. Had we not had God's grace going in, or picked it up along the way, I feel certain that after forty years of marriage, we wouldn't have much of a love story to tell. At best we'd have a "like" story, but probably it would be a "loathe" story.

Without a full measure of grace seeping its way through the pores of every moment, every comment, and every thought, even marriages that were supposedly made in heaven will end up frustrating, disappointing, and hurting the two people center stage in the wedding photos.

It doesn't matter who you are. It doesn't matter how well you were raised. It doesn't matter how much you've studied the key passages on marriage in the Bible or how many marriage conferences you've attended.

Whether you have a good marriage or one in serious need of help, when life is coming at you full throttle, you simply cannot make it work in your own power.

To have a marriage that thrives, you need grace.

The Missing Piece Is Grace

Ironically, the relationship in our life that most needs to be saturated in grace is the one in which grace is least expressed. We long to feel grace in our spouse's tone of voice, facial expressions, physical touch, and simple acts of courtesy and kindness. Yet we often show more grace to our coworkers, friends, and pets than we do to the person with whom we agreed, before witnesses, to share an underwear drawer, a bathroom mirror, and a credit card.

Marriages without grace have a way of feeling tired and old much faster than we would ever have thought going in. You can numb your disappointment with denial for a while. You can intoxicate your disillusionment with money, busyness, noble causes, and spiritual white noise. You can even agree to define mediocrity as your new normal. Without grace, our wedding day can become the overture to our song of regret.

Just ask Frank and Marci. Frank's idea of a well-spent evening is being out in his garage tinkering on one of his woodworking projects. Marci's idea of an evening well spent is a quiet house and a good book. Frank works away in the garage thinking, *One night, Marci's going to come out here with some coffee and just sit here watching me do my magic.* Marci reads away on the couch thinking, *One of these evenings, Frank's going to come in here with a good book downloaded on his iWhatever and sit next to me enjoying what I love doing the most.* They live like two people on individual islands within sight of each other, each expecting the other to row over and join their island world. You'd think after raising their kids and logging thirty-plus years of marriage together, it would be impossible for two people to become this naive—or selfish. But they did . . . and they are. And every night Marci doesn't show up in the garage and every evening Frank doesn't sit next to her on the couch drives the wedge of disappointment deeper between their hearts.

Frank and Marci are a good example of what happens when a marriage isn't filled with grace. What they need in their marriage isn't more love—they've loved each other through the ups and downs of three decades. Their love is strong and proven.

What they need is *grace*.

Every married couple will have a tough time making it without grace. That's because, at the bottom line, our marriage is too much about *us*, individually. It's about our happiness, our peace of mind, our reputation, our money, our future, our kids, our sexual needs. And when our spouse fails to meet our self-directed priorities, we feel justified to dismiss, reject, and punish them.

So, what should we do when our marriages become an obstacle course of hurt and disappointment? There are lots of marriage experts who will tell you to try harder. Maybe you've read those books or attended those marriage conferences—and you've tried many techniques to improve your marriage. But no amount of effort has resulted in lasting change in your relationship.

There are others who teach that the only way to have a successful marriage is to marry someone with whom you share much in common or do your best to find common ground. Although I don't fault someone for trying to match up the variables, I disagree with the premise. Here's why. Regardless of whom you marry and how much you share in common going in, that person is not who you're married to five years later.

And I'm not talking about divorce. I'm talking about life. You get married and (for the majority of couples) move in with each other and away from your parents. *Change.* You comingle assets or liabilities and are suddenly worth more or less than you've ever been in your lives. *Change.* You go to a delivery room or adoption courtroom and bring home a new child into your family. *Change.* Your spouse has a major medical setback. *Change.* You go to a graveyard and bury one of your parents. *Change.* Or you sit for almost forty-eight hours in the intensive-care nursery and rock one of the newborn babies your wife put in your arms . . . begging God to let that child live. I've done that. You can't help but be changed.

So what determines the level of satisfaction in marriage? To try harder? To make sure we marry someone with whom we have much in common? To try to align our mutual interests? No! Satisfaction only comes when we have *grace* to adjust to all of the highs and lows of change that life brings our way.

The Flexibility of Grace

When Bill married Heather, he thought he'd signed up for an open-ended party. Heather was spontaneous and fun and loved to laugh. If the chance for an adventure came along, she was the first to sign up. They waited four years before they had kids. During that time, Heather was everything Bill thought she would be—and much more. She especially lived up to her personality of fun and adventure when they dimmed the lights at night. Then the kids came along. Seven years and three kids later, the thrill is gone. Colicky babies, ear infections, and thousands of diapers have rubbed the excitement off Heather's face. There's no signing up for the next adventure either. Bill understands that the heavy-lifting stage of parenting can do that to you, but he wonders if this is what the future will hold for them permanently. He was going to broach the subject with Heather the other night—just after she put the last load of clothes in the washing machine and crawled into bed. But before he could say anything, Heather rolled over to him and said, "Hey, Don Juan, a newsflash for you. I'm pregnant *again*. Thanks a ton. Good night!"

Love, like anything alive, is in a constant state of motion, either growing or diminishing. The conditions we create for our love—and our responses to the hits from life—will determine whether our love thrives.

Bill and Heather love each other. But they need grace that brings encouragement, help, appreciation, and high value to their view of each other's contributions and responsibilities.

Grace is the equilibrium we apply to all the conditions and challenges that allow our marital love to improve with age. Grace is the plus sign to counter all of the negatives inherent in a partnership. Grace is the vintage agent to a covenant love that otherwise becomes flat. Grace is the dealmaker in a "till death do us part" commitment.

Grace is much more than trying harder. It's about Jesus. He's the God of grace. He's the wellspring of grace. He's the beginning, the delivery system, and the follow-through program of grace. There is no "grace-filled" without the Author of grace. Without him, all you end up with is "nice." Nice is *nice*, but it won't carry you through the deep waters of marriage. Only a heart connection with the Savior can give us the inclination and the power to reject our broken systems that work against healthy relationships. A heart connection with our spouse is a ramped-up version of the faith connection we make with God through salvation. When he is playing, on an ongoing basis, the central role he died on the cross to play, then a grace-filled marriage actually makes sense and works. Until then, our relationship is just a well-intended but misguided, and ultimately impotent, "nice."

For the record, *grace* and *nice* aren't synonyms. In fact, nice is so safe that it can actually undermine a relationship. Grace is kind enough to be forthright, accurate in assessment, and ready to take the difficult actions needed to keep love unsullied and strong—you know, the way Jesus did with the people around him every day of his public ministry. Therefore, grace can be quite gritty, as we will see in this book. But it is no less grace because it sometimes hurts when applied. And the goal of grace is always the other person . . . and their best interests.

The contradiction for the Christian is to be a willing recipient of the grace God offers us but reluctant to extend the same gift to our spouse. How ironic that the missing ingredient in our marriage when we act that way is the primary ingredient in God's heart when he deals with us.

The Context of Grace

When you pick up a book on marriage written by a Christian author you can pretty much assume that you're going to be walked through Genesis 1–3, 1 Corinthians 7, Ephesians 5:21–33, and 1 Peter 3:1–7. We're not going to do that in this book.

Although these are the four key passages that reveal the biblical "mechanics" of marriage—the leave, cleave, become one flesh, multiply a godly heritage, lead, and submit dynamics—we're not going to go there. I realize that's what a typical Christian book on marriage would do, but we're not going to do that. Two reasons: first, others have already done it as well as it can be done. I can't really add anything to their excellent insights.[1] Second, we have known people who could articulate the principles from those passages—even followed them to a tee—but you wouldn't want to have a marriage like theirs. Something was missing in their relationship that neutralized the impact the wisdom within those passages had to offer.

What I'm going to say next is very important when it comes to understanding the greater message of this book: You can get all the biblical principles of marriage right and still miss the greater point of marriage by light-years. That's because the biblical principles of marriage assume a context of God's overarching grace.[2]

Without a commitment to living out biblical principles in an atmosphere of grace, the guidelines in those passages can be turned into sledgehammers in the hands of a married person. We've seen it happen.[3] But just as the teaching in those passages represents God's desire for marriage, God's gracious example as a husband as well as his overarching teaching on grace throughout Scripture represent his empowerment for marriage. It's on this greater biblical message of applied grace and God's gracious example that we're going to camp.

Grace is what we need to create the marriage we've always longed for.

In *Grace Filled Marriage*, we'll explore the daily reality of living out a commitment to treating our spouse the way God treats us—with grace. We'll see how God's grace ends up making all the difference in the world as we navigate through the areas of sex, kids, conflict, aging, and endings . . . gracefully.

———

CHAPTER 2

Weaving Grac
Your Love Story

"Who told you?"

I wasn't sure which of Darcy's girlfriends had tipped her off. Was it Angie? She was the prime suspect in my book. Angie, with her fiery hair and innocent "I'm just minding my own business" look on her face. *You're not fooling anyone, girl!*

It couldn't have been the kids. They wouldn't rat out their own father, right? Of course they would! Come to think of it, the first thing out of their mouths when Darcy came home from her yearly trip to her mother's house was usually, "Mom, guess what Dad did while you were gone!" Our kids could make a killing as paid informants.

Darcy didn't volunteer her sources, but she did mention to me in passing that perhaps I needed some help getting the girls ready for church when she was out of town. In this case, her visit with her mother lasted long enough that I had to get the kids ready for church two Sundays in a row.

The boys weren't a problem. They were easy to get ready, with their low-maintenance haircuts. It was the girls. They both had long, thick hair. It always looked nice to me, but I'd never paid much attention ort Darcy put into making their hair look nice. That kind of me easily to her but was a mystery to me.

But on *this* visit to her mother, I had apparently outdone my eputation as the guy who had no clue when it comes to fixing little girls' hair. I didn't think it was all that important, but Darcy put this in the same category with tea parties and knowing the names of the girls' dolls. It's something a dad needed to do.

It was winter. I remember because I had built a nice fire in the fireplace. Earlier, when we were cleaning up from dinner, Darcy had mentioned that she wanted to show me something after we put the kids down . . . something that might take some time . . . something about the girls' hair.

Bedtime stories were read, prayers were prayed, and lullabies were sung. When we both made our way down the hall to the family room, four little minds were whisking their way off to dreamland. Darcy was carrying a comb and a hairbrush, which made me nervous. I started wondering if I should put on my camos or my fly fishing vest—just in case one of my buddies stopped by unannounced, wondering what I was up to. "Oh, nothing. Just looking in Darcy's hair for stuff."

I was in the process of taking a seat next to her on the couch when she said, "Why don't you put on some music? This may take a while."

I picked a station that played songs that were popular when we were in college, added logs to the fire, and then sat down next to her. She explained, "I heard you had a rough time fixing the girls' hair the past two Sundays." (It had to have been Angie.) "So I thought I'd teach you to do something with their hair that—even if you don't do a good job of it—is at least better than what you have done up to this point. I'm going to teach you how to French-braid."

"Is this necessary?" I said, worrying that I'd lose my Man Card if this got out.

Darcy assured me I'd be grateful the next time I was in charge of the girls—plus, she said, "This will be fun."

This is how I found myself sitting on the couch for a couple of hours one evening brushing out Darcy's hair and trying over and over to get the process right. She was sitting cross-legged on the floor, my knees straddling her, as I brushed her hair, separated it, and—following her instructions—wove the strands down the back of her head. After a half-dozen tries, I started to get the hang of it. Finally, it was starting to look as if it might just pass muster for the two little Kimmel girls.

For most of that evening, Darcy and I were both quiet—I was trying to figure out what I was supposed to do while Darcy stared into the fire and listened to the music. It was one of those nice just-the-two-of-us memories in the making that come along in marriage. The best ones are usually unplanned.

As we sat there with the fire, the music, and me trying to figure out how to be a more effective father of daughters, the experience took on more meaning when a song came on the radio.

Neither of us had heard it in a long while, but it struck a familiar and agreeable chord. Music does that—especially music attached to a specific time in your life. When this song had been part of the rotation of Top 40 radio stations, Darcy and I were just solidifying our commitment to each other. So as soon as I heard the guitar introduction, I knew I would enjoy the next few minutes.

It was an old Carole King song called "You've Got a Friend"—James Taylor's version. I couldn't remember the last time I'd heard it, but some voices wear like a good pair of boots. JT's was one of them for me. But there was another reason I warmed to this song. For me, the lyrics also sang like a hymn about Jesus being there for us. Jesus, our ever-present, always-ready Savior, showed us how much he cared about the gritty issues of our life by making them his gritty issues. No matter what, no matter when, no matter why . . . he is ready to step up and be there, not only as God, but as our Savior as well. Jesus said he'd be there as our friend (John 15:15) winter, spring, summer, or fall. So as James Taylor sang, I hummed along as I worked a new braid down the back of Darcy's head.

There are times when I think God is trying to teach me something important. This was one of those times. Suddenly the words of the song and the braid in Darcy's hair came together in one grand, tender *aha!* This realization jarred me in such a way that I turned down the corner of this page of our life so that I could revisit it often.

When you look at a woman's braided hair, it appears that two strands of hair are overlapping each other from the top to the bottom. It looks like *two* . . . but I was holding *three* in my hand. As I thought of that friend we have in Jesus—and Darcy and me trying to figure out life, parenting, and love together—it hit me that perhaps the bigger reason this evening happened had more to do with God and us than with my ability to get my daughters looking presentable to the public.

A grace-filled marriage is more about weaving together three people than it is joining together a man and a woman.

Braiding Your Story with God's Love

The Bible says that in marriage, the two shall become one. But God also wants those two to be one with him. In grace-filled marriages, three lives weave together to look like two, presenting themselves as one complete and beautiful braid.

And so it is with *you*. When you and your spouse got married, God's design was to braid your love and hopes and dreams for each other together with *his*. He wanted to slip among the two of you and weave his grace into your love story. You may not have realized how much you needed God's grace going in, but the more you live and the more your love is tested, the more you know how desperately the two of you require his tender, strengthening touch.

Your marriage needs to be filled with God's grace for those times:

- When your challenges stack up against you, but you've run out of ideas.
- When you hold fast to that opinion you swear is right, when deep down you know you're dead wrong.
- When you've been making love so little because you've been fighting so much.
- When you can't figure out how to live with each other, but you don't want to find out what it's like to live without each other.
- When the demands of kids, work, time, and money have exhausted your resolve.
- When you have no one to turn to and nothing to hang on to but each other—and God.

Grace wants to lead the way when it comes to processing our disappointments and helping us through the darkest moments of our marriage. It needs to be the active ingredient of our marriage covenant. But sometimes it's hard to see what you don't have. And while most of us would love to weave God's grace into our love story, we're not sure exactly how it fits.

To have a grace-filled marriage, first we need to recognize the graceless ways we tend to view our spouse. Then we will learn how to replace those distorted views with a grace-filled perspective.

With this in mind, I'd like to use a multigenerational story to introduce the three most common graceless perspectives we often maintain toward our spouse. I'd like you to meet Rick, Mia, and Rick's dad.

Family Business

At first glance, you'd figure Mia to be the kind of woman most men would enjoy introducing as their wife. Without a backstage pass to catch a glimpse behind their public facade, you'd think she and Rick enjoyed a lot of passion and laughs. They were a couple you'd want on your short list of folks to hang out with. In my line of work, however, I get handed the backstage pass almost immediately.

I found out that Rick was having a tough time smiling about his marriage. It had to do with Mia's ongoing critiques of him. Over the years she had become extremely disappointed. As a result, she had developed a sophisticated ability to use her words like daily kicks to Rick's groin.

It all revolved around Rick's dad. Here's the short version: Rick's grandfather had developed a successful business. He also intended it to be the family business. When Rick's father was old enough, he accepted it from Rick's grandfather out of obligation rather than inclination. Which explains why Rick's most prominent memories of his childhood were of his father whining about his pathetic, wasted life.

When it was Rick's turn to take the mantel of the family business from his father, he decided he'd rather have his eyebrows surgically removed than follow in his father's footsteps. When college was over, Rick made two major decisions: first, to tell his father he was not going to work with him, and second, to take Mia as his wife.

Most of the time, a .500 batting average isn't bad. But Rick's decision to tell his father to "Take this job and . . . "—well, find someone else to pass it on to—turned his father into a toxic extension of his and Mia's relationship. Even though his dad lived hours away and hardly had any face time with Rick and Mia, it was as though he was at every meal, on every car ride, and sleeping between them every night.

Here's how this worked. Rick's father was a high-controlling nightmare.[1] He refused to extend to his son the blessing all children long for from their father, and he used Rick's longing for that blessing as a way to manipulate him through guilt and shame.[2]

Rick and Mia's toxic encounters with Rick's dad were limited. But the effect of Rick not feeling like he measured up colored his view of himself so much that it was as though he were living with a debilitating handicap. His father-wound paralyzed his ability to be confident as a husband and father. Mia started out sympathetic. She carried the metaphorical pom-poms as she encouraged Rick through their early years of marriage. But like a cheerleader for a lousy high school football team, by the fourth quarter, she began to think, *What's the point?*

Two things disappointed Mia the most. She was hurt by how self-absorbed Rick had become as a result of his toxic relationship with his dad. He centered everything in their life (not just the issues with his dad) on how it impacted *him*. The second thing that bothered her was his refusal to get over it.

"Listen," she told him one day, "it's a tragic but simple truth. Your dad isn't going to give you his blessing. He's a self-absorbed, bitter man who didn't get a blessing from his own father. It's time to grieve it, accept the obvious, and move on with your life. It would have been nice, but the reality is you don't need his approval to be all that you were intended to be, and all that the kids and I *need* you to be. You've already got it. It happened on a cross a long time ago. Jesus has already given you his blessing, and that's better than anything a parent could give. I need you to accept what you've got and stop waiting for what's never coming."

Usually you have to pay tons of money to hear that kind of blunt, spot-on honesty from a professional, God-fearing shrink. But Rick didn't take her advice. That's what happens when you're focused on yourself. Mia figured if she was going to stay sane, she would have to develop a separate life within their marital partnership. She threw herself into her kids, fitness, church, and hobbies. She resigned herself to the fact that her passive husband required her to wear the bra *and* the boxers in this marriage—whether she liked it or not. Their victories as a couple were few, their passion intermittent, and their laughs eons apart.

Oh, one more thing. If you were to stop by the home of Rick's dad to give him a piece of your mind for being such a difficult father, you'd find a Bible-reading, Scripture-quoting, praying man who can't for the life of him figure out why his son is so angry. He'd outline for you all the ways he sacrificed to give Rick a jump-start on life; how he prays for Rick *daily* that God will help him step up to his role as a man, a husband, a father . . . and a son. If you met Rick's father, you'd think Rick had made this all up.

But he didn't.

A Matter of Perspective

The three people in this story have something in common with you and me: they're looking at each other through lenses. Much like eyeglasses, these metaphorical lenses we all look through frame our thinking and determine how we interpret what we see. Sometimes that perspective is imposed on us through the way we were raised or through our difficult experiences. Other times it's just our lens of choice. Regardless, like windows to the world around us, these starting points in our thinking often decide the conclusions we draw about ourselves, others, love, and God.

So what happens if the lens you're looking through is distorted or flawed? Obviously, you end up with a distorted and flawed perspective.

That's what couples do. We don't have an option as to *whether* we're looking through a lens. We only have a choice as to *which* one. I could list several, but in this chapter, I will limit our discussion to the three most common flawed and distorted marital lenses. One might be the primary lens of choice that determines your perspective. But like people who carry different glasses with them for different demands, you might have access to all three lenses for whichever accommodates your need at the moment.

To track with me, I want you to picture an oval piece of glass about eighteen inches wide and twelve inches high. It's the lens a spouse chooses to look through and frame the perspective of the husband or wife on the other side.

The Me Lens

For this oval, I want you to picture the kind of glass they use in police interrogation rooms—you know, the kind that's tinted on one side but mirrored on the other. Etched across it is the word *Me*. This is the kind of lens Rick was holding in front of him (mirror side facing him). His attitude toward everything happening in his marriage was determined by how it reflected on him. And everyone looking at him through his Me Lens could see just how selfish he truly was.

His was a life of personal pronouns attached to words that were supposed to be team concepts: my needs, my time, my money, my kids, my plans, my future, my rest, my space, my stuff, and my house. What he didn't realize (until I mentioned it to him) was that he had chosen a path that not only *guaranteed* he would not enjoy the grace God meant for him and Mia to experience in their marriage, but it would also incur God's pushback toward any of his self-absorbed efforts. Don't take my word for it. Look what James, one of the writers of the New Testament, says: "God opposes the proud, but gives grace to the humble" (James 4:6 ESV).

Self-absorbed people are the converse of humility. They short-circuit God's desire to pour grace over them.

But Rick was simply standing in a crowd of people who look through the Me Lens. In fact, this is the lens that Rick, you, and I were *born* looking through. Children come from their mother's womb focused on themselves, their needs, and their wants. When you hear a baby's cry, it's a gigantic *me*! "I'm hungry!" "I'm lonely!" "I'm scared!" "I'm wet!" Once toddlers can verbalize their feelings, that "me" often morphs into "mine!"

Then we grow up and get married. Our natural tendency toward self-focus is why shrewd pastors require couples to exchange the traditional wedding vows or a poetic equivalent of them. There's a reason those particular vows have lasted so long. The wise originator of them realized that for a marriage to thrive, both spouses have to declare an outward focus on the needs and best interests of the person they're marrying—an attitude that is counterintuitive to the way they were born. "I take you as you are with all your issues from this day forward regardless of your performance, health, or earning power, whether in good times or bad, ready or not, here we go," or something like that. These vows assume the inevitable challenges that any two self-oriented people are sure to face once they sign the marriage license and put the wedding reception in their rearview mirror.

Of course, vowing to accept our spouse with their unique issues doesn't mean we won't try to help our spouse harness their deeper potential. A good marriage should help both spouses improve their contribution to the big picture of life. Bringing an "I believe in you" type of love to our marriage commitment can help our spouse spruce up their personal and professional life or maintain their strength and health. However, this isn't done with condemnation. It's not even done for our sake. It's making a commitment of our love to bring out the best in our spouse.

Unfortunately, the Me Lens negates all of that. In the process, it wearies the spouse on the receiving end. Like Mia, you get tired of hoping, praying, and working for what appears to be a lost cause. Next thing you know, all you see when you look at your spouse is what annoys you most about them. Rick's insistence on holding the Me Lens in front of him was snuffing out any light God was trying to shine through him.

The apostle Paul explains why the Me Lens is the antithesis of how we should look at life:

Do nothing out of selfish ambition or vain conceit. Rather, in humility value others above yourselves, not looking to your own interests but each of you to the interests of others (Philippians 2:3–4).

These verses tell us what we *shouldn't* do and then what we *should* do when it comes to other people. Don't let selfish ambition (like trying to get a closed-hearted father to give you the blessing he's not inclined to give) and vain conceit (like thinking your disappointments are so worthy of your focus that you're justified in throwing your wife and kids under the same bus your father threw you under). Meanwhile, *do* keep your selfish ego in check and value others as more important than yourself.

This passage teaches us how we should deal with the people God puts in our life—including our spouse. But it isn't advice in a vacuum. A few verses down, Paul unpacks the reason for the "shouldn't" and the "should." In fact, he goes to the very heart of God to make his case: "In your relationships with one another, have the same mindset as Christ Jesus: Who, being in very nature God, did not consider equality with God something to be used to his own advantage; rather, he made himself nothing, by taking the very nature of a servant, being made in human likeness. And being found in appearance as a man, he humbled himself by becoming obedient to death—even death on a cross!" (vv. 5–8).

Paul's argument for why we shouldn't stare through the Me Lens is that Jesus didn't—even though he actually had the right to. Take this in with me for a minute. The *one person* in the entire universe who is entitled to focus on himself is God. He alone, with his holiness, unblemished righteousness, and unfettered power deserves humankind's praise. But Jesus didn't consider all the privileges of his deity something he had to hold on to at all costs. Why? Because he saw a huge need in humankind that could only be met by him humbly setting aside his divine privileges (not his deity) and lowering himself to humanity's level for a time in order to suffer and die for our sins. All God expects us to do for each other is what he was willing to first do for us.

A Me Lens perspective insults the very nature of God's heart. It tries to justify itself by saying, "You don't understand. I've been maligned, mistreated, and shortchanged by people who should know better. It's not fair what life has served up to me, so I'm justified in my self-absorption." And God replies, "Really? You've been maligned, mistreated, and shortchanged by people who should know better? Welcome to my world." Yet God, in his grace, chooses to focus on our needs and best interests, regardless of the cost to him.

Whether you are looking through the Me Lens because you were born that way, bent that way by how you were raised, or maligned into it, it's a prescription for misery for everyone around the dinner table. Rick lived it, Mia felt it, and their whole family suffered because of it.

So how about you? How often do you drop the Me Lens between you and your spouse? I know for me, looking through the Me Lens would be second nature had Jesus not decided to do something about my sin nature. Thanks to him, you and I and guys like Rick have a better alternative. But then there's Mia . . .

The Love If Lens

For this lens I'd like you to picture a smoky, tinted oval with the words *Love If* etched on it. This is the one Mia most often looked through when she considered Rick. Her view of him was dimmed by her disappointments, her blocked expectations, his broken promises, and her father-in-law.

The Love If Lens is often a reaction to things you feel you must manipulate in order to survive. You don't have to, in reality, but enough setbacks to your relationships and enough success at getting what you want through conditional love inclines you to keep the Love If Lens in front of you through the highs and lows of marital love.

If anything, the Love If Lens represents a typical brand of love, the kind that comes with strings attached. It says, "I'll love you if you do these things:

- Start speaking kindly to me and stop criticizing me."
- Make my load lighter when you come home from work."
- Take an active role in the kids' daily responsibilities."
- Assume some spiritual leadership in our family."
- Find me more interesting than your hobbies."
- Appear as if you actually have a spiritual pulse."

"Love If" is a conjoined twin to "Love When." This kind of lens says things like "My love, tenderness, and kindness will show up more often when you finally decide to stop nitpicking my life." Or "I'll give you that passionate sex you desire when you stop hanging out with your loser friends." The reasons this lens shows up might be based on legitimate issues that need to be dealt with, but they're still conditions that block the person on the other side from feeling loved regardless of their performance.

The excuses we make for limiting our love are similar to the ones we make from behind the Me Lens. It's a self-serving, self-protecting starting point that makes marital love more of a contest than a covenant. This scorekeeping kind of love gives rewards for straight A's but feels justified in holding back kindness and respect for average, or less than average, performances.

Aren't you glad that isn't the way God deals with you and me?

Some of you reading this may be saying, "What do you mean, Tim? I thought this *is* the way God deals with me."

Before we go any further in our discussion on graceless perspectives, let me address something important: Many followers of Jesus assume God's love is based on their performance. They think God will love them more if they jump through the right spiritual hoops and less if they behave badly. That's why they feel justified in holding up the Love If Lens between them and their spouse.

Let's be crystal clear on an eternal reality: if God extended conditional love to us, then divine affection would completely stop moving in our direction. That's because "there is no one righteous, not even one" (Romans 3:10), and "all our righteous acts are like filthy rags" (Isaiah 64:6) when compared with God's holy perfection. Furthermore, the Scriptures teach us, "He does not treat us as our sins deserve or repay us according to our iniquities" (Psalm 103:10). If he had, we'd all be dead. God relates to us through the finished work of Christ on the cross as the substitute sacrifice for our sins.

The apostle Paul makes it clear that God does not withhold his love from us or dispense it to us based on conditions: "Neither death nor life, neither angels nor demons, neither the present nor the future, nor any powers, neither height nor depth, nor anything else in all creation [including ourselves and our boneheaded behavior], will be able to separate us from the love of God that is in Christ Jesus our Lord" (Romans 8:38–39).

Does God withhold his *blessing* or his *privilege* based on our behavior? Of course he does, just as we do with our kids when they misbehave. Withholding certain blessings or privileges as a result of unacceptable actions is part of responsible relationships. But does God ever withhold his *love*? Nope. No way. No how. Regardless of how we behave, he loves us completely.

That's why Mia's insistence on letting her Love If Lens frame her response to Rick has no defense. It's a response that is completely foreign to the heart of God. God doesn't deal with Mia that way, so she has no grounds for thinking she can put strings on her love for Rick. Come to think of it, neither do we when we look at our spouse through a Love If Lens. We may have a long list of reasons we feel justified in maintaining a Love If attitude toward our spouse, but none of them hold water when we compare our attitude to the perspective God maintains toward us. You could say, "Yeah, Tim, but he's God. We're flawed human beings." True and true. But he's in the business of indwelling us, transforming us, and freeing us from the sin that so easily entangles us. More than anything else, the lenses we hold up are not determined by fate, but determined by us. We just have to decide.

The Pious Lens

Which brings me to Rick's father. For him, I want you to picture a stained-glass oval with the word *Pious* etched on it. Of the three lenses, this one is the most sinister. That's because most people can be convinced of their self-absorption or self-protection, but it's much harder to get people to acknowledge their self-righteousness. They're convinced that God ordains their behavior, and they've got the chapters and verses to back it up. They also have the well-worn Bible, tear-covered prayer list, and sometimes the pastor's endorsement to prove they're right and you're wrong.

Jesus had to contend with these kinds of people all the time. They had a biblical black belt in superiority and used it to deliver roundhouse kicks to him at every turn. Of course with him they met their match . . . and then some. Their verbal blows didn't faze Jesus' resolve, even when their influence was behind the blows of the hammer driving nails into his hands and feet. Still, Jesus made it clear that their pious poison was unacceptable. He called them snakes (Matthew 23:33), whitewashed tombs (Matthew 23:27), and kissing cousins of the devil himself (John 8:44).

Obviously, I'm a fan of well-worn Bibles and tear-stained prayer lists—if these are in the hands of humble, gracious followers of Jesus. But we all know there is a huge difference between folks whose faith is an extension of God's heart and those whose faith is an extension of their egos. The biggest stains on Christian history have come from people who were hearers of God's Word but not doers, deceiving themselves in the process (James 1:22). In fact, self-deception occupies the La-Z-Boy in these people's hearts. They listen to highly skilled preachers, love the richness of vibrant worship, and enjoy the trademark people within a Christian community. But everything runs through a self-serving filter that catches what props up their ego and ignores or attacks the stuff designed to convict their heart of sin, righteousness, and judgment.

Rick's father is what you get when you confine God's grace to the lost/found–blind/see work of salvation but don't want that same grace transforming and tenderizing your heart toward the people God has called you to love. Unfortunately, this happens all the time within the community of faith, and Rick's dad was a card-carrying member of this group. He was a self-righteous man who used his knowledge of the Bible to try to control his son with spiritual guilt and shame. When Rick attempted to defend himself with that same Bible, his father was arrogantly dismissive toward him.

Shattered Lenses and a New Perspective

Regardless of which lens was held up, the person holding it didn't feel more loved. And the family member on the receiving end of each distorted point of view could never enjoy the heart connection they longed for. That's what happens when we frame our relationships with an unreliable perspective. And that's why the best thing to do with these lenses is to take a hammer to them.

Rick, Mia, and Rick's dad may seem familiar to you. They may remind you of the branches in your own family tree . . . or of people sitting next to you in this year's Christmas photo . . . or of the person who stares back at you in the mirror each morning.

When Darcy and I married, we had each packed all three of these lenses to take with us on our honeymoon. For years, we kept them within arm's length, at the ready. We became pros at moving from a Me Lens to a Love If Lens to a Pious Lens—sometimes within the same exchange of selfishness.

But like Rick and Mia, we eventually found our way out. That's right: Rick and Mia are no longer stuck where they were for so many years of their marriage. They hit a flash point in their relationship where they realized that if they didn't change something, their marriage was over. Two things happened. First, they both owned up to the distorted lenses they were holding in front of themselves as they viewed each other. They recognized the hurt and bitterness that reflected off these lenses and directly into the heart of their mate. They admitted the reality that all of these distorted, graceless lenses had nothing to do with the best interests of their spouse and everything to do with their own self-protection. This owning up involved confession, forgiveness, and accountability as Rick and Mia decided to set aside those lenses, hopefully for good. Second, they picked up a different lens: clean, clear, and with a divine focus. This lens's perspective was all about the best interests of the one being viewed through it rather than the one holding it. It was the Grace Lens. They got it directly from the nail-scarred hand of God's only begotten Son. This fresh, freeing, grace-filled perspective brought new energy, respect, contentment, and passion to a relationship that had been steeped in disappointment.

Rick's dad still has his Pious Lens stapled to his forehead. But his attempts at missile-guided manipulation don't work on Rick anymore. Neither does his refusal to give Rick his blessing define Rick and Mia's relationship. In fact, their commitment to embrace God's grace as a way of life has turned their attitude toward Rick's dad from menacing to ministry. It couldn't have come at a better time. Rick's dad's health is starting to fail. So is his mother's. It's going to fall to Rick and Mia to oversee their twilight care. Rick and Mia are committed to treating their parents the same way God treats them—with grace, kindness, and love, regardless of whether it's deserved or returned. And they're not expecting their parents to have some grace epiphany as they slip into the two-minute warning of life. That's okay, though. They simply want to love their parents the way God has loved them.

How about you? Are you viewing your spouse through the Me Lens, the Love If Lens, or the Pious Lens? Have you—like Rick and Mia, and Darcy and me—been slipping these distorted lenses between you and the person you love whenever it serves your best interests . . . regardless of the price your spouse has to pay in the process? If so, I hope you'll stick around for the adventure.

Help and hope is on the way. There is a place where God's grace can be lived out through your marriage, and you're going to find it where it's always been—near to the heart of God.

—

CHAPTER 3

A Grace-Filled Perspective

—

Grace doesn't add up.

This probably explains why most couples shy away from making grace the default mode of their relationships. It's counterintuitive. Intimidating too. Grace is so . . . selfless. We prefer the simple math behind the cause-effect dynamic within relationships. You scratch my back: I'll scratch yours. You nick my car; I'll burn down your garage.

Sometimes we can't help but double down on payback if what we lost was close to our heart. Human math works like that. It assumes the right to add on to our spouse's tab for pain, suffering, or stupidity. For instance, if you take something that wasn't yours to take, like your spouse's dreams for the future, your spouse may feel justified holding the debt over your head indefinitely. "It's only *fair*," your spouse may say.

When two people start on a life journey together, and one doesn't hold up their end of the itinerary, the one having to carry the bulk of the marital luggage assumes they're entitled to be bitter for as long as it helps them cope. It's how relational ledgers are kept. The short-changed spouse feels they have the right to withhold niceties until the other person gets their act together. It seems less complicated if we keep a relationship scorecard in our head . . . and our heart. Here are a few examples.

You sit there listening to the preacher talk about "joy." Just because he dresses like the cover of *GQ* and preaches from an app on his tablet doesn't make his words sound less hollow. He hasn't spent a day, let alone the past two years, with the woman sitting next to you. If he had, he'd rethink his main point. It was just one poor decision that cost you your savings nest egg. The opportunity seemed right at the time. You agreed you should have consulted your wife. You acknowledged that the bulk of the money was from what she brought to the marriage, and you had no right to spend it without her signing off. You took all the blame. You ate a buffet of crow. And you've been working your rear off at a second job to replace it. But that was *two years* ago, yet she holds it over you as if it happened yesterday.

You wonder why they call them "pink slips." It wasn't pink. It was a white paper with stark black printing. As you signed it, the HR rep had the gall to suggest that the severance package was "generous when you factor in the overall economy." Sorry, but there's a Grand Canyon between a severance package and an ongoing salary. You never felt as low as you did when you walked in from the garage carrying that box filled with the stuff from your cubicle. The one time . . . the *one stinking time* you needed your wife to pull you close, hold you tight, and assure you that she believed in you, she just stood there, arms crossed, staring at the floor. You understood why she was scared. Heck, you were scared. But you didn't do anything wrong. You weren't fired; you were just a victim of downsizing. Her lack of support since then keeps gnawing at you.

You think how ironic that "lol" now seems.[1] It was the last thing you texted before the right tire slipped off the edge of the asphalt, and you and your infant smashed into the fence. The baby didn't get a scratch. She didn't even cry. But your husband won't let it go. He holds on to his anger. He took away your car keys and cell phone as if you were a reckless teenager. It would be one thing if this was yesterday. But it was a month ago. There's been no kindness and no sex since. Just punishment and doubt about your fitness as a mother. All because of one poorly timed "lol."

You watch your husband sit there staring at the TV, seeing nothing. He left a proud warrior, but he came home a shadow of who he once was. A uniform covered with medals from his commanding officers doesn't change the reality that he's just a shell of the man you married. He led men into some of the toughest engagements a soldier could imagine, without so much as a powder burn, but he came home with his emotions in a body bag. The doctor said the PTSD was treatable. The army was good to their word in working with him. But you wonder if this is going to be your new standard.

Regardless of how much relational capital a couple has going into their marriage, if they keep a balance sheet on each other's behavior, the *addition* of one person's downside will *subtract* from the other person's level of commitment, *multiply* their frustrations with each other, and ultimately *divide* their hearts. Once again, this shows how we all desperately need God's grace.

Divine Math

Fortunately, God doesn't keep score the way we do. If he did, none of us would still be standing. We'd be gone, nada, over, kaput. Nor does he maintain a relationship with us that is remotely close to the score-keeping arrangement we maintain with each other. That's not his style because that's not his heart. God deals with us from his overwhelming grace:

- He's empathetic and understanding when all we can muster is fear and doubt (Romans 8:15; 2 Timothy 1:7; Hebrews 4:15–16).
- He sees us for what we can be instead of judging us for what we are (Luke 15:21–22; John 8:10–11).
- He imputes value in us long after we feel we don't have any left (Romans 5:8).
- He reaches down to us at our lowest to lift us up to his highest (Psalm 40:2; Habakkuk 3:17–19; Romans 5:6).
- He unleashes his mercy and hope in order to rescue us when we're at our worst (Ephesians 2:4–7; Philippians 2:5–8).
- He measures our sins against the backdrop of his far greater love for us (Romans 8:1–4).
- He takes our naked sin and clothes it in his forgiveness (Psalm 32:1–2; Romans 13:14; Galatians 3:27).
- He takes our shame and washes it clean with his sacrifice (Psalm 51:12; Isaiah 1:18; Romans 3:23–24).
- He rescues us from that sin and shame, even at the expense of his own life (Romans 8:31–33).

And therein lies our problem when it comes to our marriage.

God doesn't treat us the way we typically treat each other. Yet if we've placed our faith in Christ and his transforming work on the cross, we should be filled with grace as we relate to our spouse—especially when it comes to the actions and attitudes that would otherwise erode our commitment to each other. If we're in Christ, and he is in us, then we should treat each other the way he treats us—with grace. If we truly grasped God's gracious love and let him implant that same kind of love in our hearts, we'd run out of superlatives trying to verbalize the amazing love and peace he would bring to our marriage.

Why Many Aren't Quick to Embrace God's Grace

The average married couple who has put their faith in Jesus rarely comes close to the purpose, meaning, and victory God wants us to experience. He wants us to experience this even during the greatest challenges we face as couples. But most of the time we go through marriage without understanding what we have in Christ, who we are in Christ, and what his work on our behalf at Calvary means to our relationship with each other. This can even happen with couples who know and are committed to the major biblical teachings on marriage roles.

Let me offer a suggestion as to why this is. Maybe it's because most Christians don't actually "get" grace.[2] I don't mean we haven't received God's grace. We just don't fully grasp what it's all about. If we did, on a grand scale, our churches would be more influential, our marriages would be more resilient, and we'd be sending a more passionate generation of Jesus followers into the future. Oh, we *get* the part about "I once was lost but now am found"—that we're morally bankrupt and can't get into heaven without God's intervening grace—but we don't get the part of how the grace that saved us can also redefine us and transform how we treat others, especially in our marriage.

Our marriage can't come close to what it could be until we accept Christ's work as it truly is, on his gracious terms. Until then, we'll always struggle to extend grace to our spouse. It's hard to give what we struggle to receive. More than anything else, our desire is that you grow to understand the depth, breadth, and height of God's amazing grace, and then from that understanding choose to embrace this grace as the defining factor of your relationship with your spouse.

When Darcy and I got married, we had no idea how selfish we were coming in. But marriage forced us to read the fine print about what was required of us if we wanted to make this sharing-our-stuff, surrendering-our-space, thinking-of-the-other-person-ahead-of-ourselves arrangement actually work. We found ourselves at a crossroads. Fortunately, at that crossroads, we had a clear line of sight to the cross.

God's Grace—A New Way of Looking at Each Other

So far we've discussed three lenses: the Me Lens, the Love If Lens, and the Pious Lens. Let's examine a better alternative: the Grace Lens. Picture a pure, clear oval piece of glass in front of you with the simple but poignant word *Grace* etched across it. It's a perspective that comes directly from God's heart. This is the lens he chooses to look through when he considers you and me.

If we've put our faith in Christ, we each have a choice. It can't be made based on our spouse's actions. It must be based on God's actions. Christ did something wonderful for us so that we could be something wonderful for the person we married. What he did wasn't an act of love to be admired but a sacrificial gift to be embraced, enjoyed, and shared. He gave us grace. He didn't offer it to us with strings attached, but he did offer it with his almighty power attached. His grace can give us the power to override our self-absorbed ego, to overcome our self-protection tendencies, and to overwhelm our self-righteous piety. The power of Christ's work on the cross offers the only alternative to our inclination to hold the smug Me Lens, the sly Love If Lens, or the sinister Pious Lens between us and the person we wake up next to each day.

But there's more. God's grace is sufficient for us, not just because he chose to make grace the delivery system of his forgiveness, but also because he chose to make grace the foundation of his own marriage to you and me. Of course! Grace-filled marriages come from the grace-filled union we have with the God of the universe. God wants us to enjoy our marriage here on earth because he's already guaranteed us one in heaven . . . to him and with him! This is a whole other dimension of the grace story. For a deeper understanding of it, let's consider it in the context of a marriage proposal.

Romancing the Stone

Marriage proposals are as old as time and as new as fresh-baked love. These "Let's get the ball rolling and *do* this thing!" preludes to weddings cover the gamut from a personal request in a quiet corner to a flash mob with a cast of thousands.

I've seen marriage proposals at restaurants, watched cheesy attempts on stadium Jumbotrons, and observed a few proposals orchestrated by conscripted travelers in airports. They're either planned with Facebook in mind, or nothing but the answer in mind, yet they play a huge part in what follows. They're the equivalent of the national anthem before a sporting event. Nothing can happen until someone sings the song or, in this case, drops to one knee.

I encouraged our sons to take the private route when they popped the question, and I asked our daughters to expect the same. A decision like giving your heart to someone for as long as you live is tough enough to make without onlookers leveraging the scene toward a particular outcome. I think decisions like these are best made in a context where the person being asked has the freedom to say no. So, for the Kimmels at least, the requests and the answers were made in private.

But private doesn't mean you still can't make it a beautiful moment when you pull out an engagement ring. Ian proposed to our daughter, Shiloh, under a bridge in downtown Phoenix. Years before, his high school had held their senior prom against this backdrop. He had tucked this romantic location away for future reference, and when his heart was ready to ask Shiloh to cast her lot with him, he arranged for her to meet him there, where he quietly and tenderly asked her to marry him.

Our son Cody is very determined, like me, and really smart, like his mother. He was certain he wanted to take on life with a sweet Texas girl named Lauren by his side. This provoked him to write one hundred haikus and have them bound into a book, which he gave her at an isolated bench in the shadow of the Texas State Capitol. It was a blustery evening when the two of them met at "their bench" on the capitol grounds—a bench on which they had spent hours talking and dreaming about their future. He dropped to one knee, read her a couple of poems, pulled out the ring, and asked her the question.

I had to look up *haiku* on the Internet when they called to tell us their big news. He had spent months prior to this crescendo writing one hundred Japanese-style poems about his love for her. I thought, *Are you nuts? What are all your buddies supposed to do when it's their turn to ask a girl to marry them?* Maybe I should have advised Cody to propose in a way that didn't set the bar so high for everyone else.

I was committed to keeping the bar low when I asked Darcy for her hand. It was New Year's Day. I stopped by her house just before the Rose Bowl kickoff on television.

I planned to make my move during halftime. When the big moment came, Michigan was leading Stanford 3–0. Darcy had been sitting beside me throughout the first half with her arm through mine while playing footsie with me on the hassock. You can't get any more romantic than this. It's these kinds of moments that bring tears to guys in sports bars across the land.

I pulled out the ring box, opened it (grab your hankies, men), and asked if she'd be interested in taking our relationship to the concierge level. She put on the ring and said, "Yes!" We hugged, and then she stood up, kissed me, and went to find her mom to show her the ring. Only after she'd walked out did I remember the get-down-on-one-knee thing. I figured it was probably more of an option than a requirement. I watched the remainder of the game with a smile on my face. Stanford won. It's the stuff epic movies are made of.

The Cause and Effect of Proposals and Weddings

It doesn't matter how elaborate or simple a proposal is when it comes to predicting the success of the marriage that follows. The same goes for weddings. Whether you pull off the wedding of the century or pull up to a drive-through chapel window in Vegas, it doesn't determine the depth and richness of your marriage. Marital success is far more in the hands or more specifically, the hearts of the people popping questions and exchanging vows. Proposals and weddings are only as predictable as the couples making the commitments.

This is why we need something bigger and better going for us than what we typically have to offer. We all have a threshold we reach sooner than we could imagine. Once there, the best we have to tap into is used up. We all need grace to guide our marriages. Engagements and weddings are nice, but they aren't the tests of our resolve like marriage is.

Think of the things that cause you disappointment in your marriage:

- Your spouse's annoying habits—or their lack of good habits
- The way your spouse views money—or the way they spend it
- Their preoccupation with the kids—or lack of interest in them
- Their need to be early to events—or their consistent tardiness
- Their fastidiousness—or sloppiness
- How quickly they explode when frustrated—or how quickly they retreat to avoid conflict
- How often they'd prefer having sex—or how often they'd prefer *not* to have sex
- How much they depend on you—or how little they factor you into their life
- The way they easily default to tears—or the fact you've never seen them cry
- How preoccupied they are with church—or how little they're interested in church

These are some points of frustration Darcy and I have heard spouses voice over the years. If it was just an every-once-in-a-while kind of issue, most couples could manage their way through these. But when they're day-after-day occurrences, these annoyances start to grate on us. Even the best of us can fall into the nitpicking trap.

Credit Card Focus

Suppose I took a credit card out of my wallet, held it up in the air, and said, "This credit card represents what it is about your spouse that drains the joy out of your relationship." Now imagine I hold this credit card sideways between my thumb and index finger, take a few steps back from you, extend my arm, and then look at you. Can I see you? The answer of course is yes. Although the credit card takes up some space at the end of my extended arm, I can still take in the big picture of who you are.

Now suppose I pull my arm in close and hold that same credit card just an inch from my eyes. Can I still see you? The answer is no. Did the credit card change size? No. It's still as small as it always was, but because of how closely I'm holding it to my eyes, it's all I can see.

In the same way, the things about our spouse that annoy us or frustrate us may be quite small in the grand scheme of life. Yet if the annoyance is all we focus on, it's all we'll see. Some of the things that annoy us about our spouse are simply the tail side of their personality strength (social people tend to struggle with punctuality, organized people often want to arrive early, and so on). Other things that annoy us come from factors imposed on our spouse from their parents (such as poor role models when it comes to money or parenting or handling conflict). Sometimes we're annoyed by something about our spouse that isn't necessarily wrong, just different from what we'd prefer.

Regardless, if we choose to focus on these things, then our spouse doesn't stand a chance. They may be trying hard to remedy these points of annoyance. It doesn't matter. What they truly are or what they actually do is irrelevant. If we choose to focus on the credit-card-size things that bug us most about them, it's *impossible* for them to measure up. This marital cruelty supplants commitment. Joy and contentment leave the scene.

A Marriage Proposal on a Cross

This brings me back to our discussion on marriage proposals. Most people would think a public execution is a lousy place to ask someone to marry you. But that's where God chose to make his intentions known to you and me. The Bible is clear that the cross is where Jesus bought our salvation with his blood. But there was something else, something rich, deep, and private that Jesus was also doing. It was there that he popped the question to his bride, the church.

Instead of getting down on one knee, he was raised up on a cross. Instead of offering an engagement ring, he offered his hands and feet to cold, cruel spikes. Instead of having folks ready to pop corks, he had an angry mob, smug clergy, and fair-weather friends who abandoned him. But he gladly did it because he was so in love with the church.

His death was the dowry for you and me. And he was the only one who could pay it. To create a marriage between the God of the universe and the riffraff of the church required some advance exchange of value to get the bride ready. We required more than a new hairdo, French nails, and a few visits to a tanning booth. No, the bride of Christ would need a new heart, a new life. So Jesus died that we might live. When he cried out, "It is finished," you and I were on his mind. He wasn't looking at us as we are, calculating our shortcomings with the backdrop of our letdowns, excuses, and betrayals. He was seeing us for what we could be in heart partnership with him as a result of the "paid in full" stamp his sacrifice placed over our sin.

Our marriage to Jesus through salvation was the ultimate name change: sinner to saint, loser to victor, slave to free, filthy to clean, guilty to forgiven. Jesus dwarfed our best haiku. As he hung there, he was seeing us differently than we see ourselves. His promises spoke through the pain, the shame, and the isolation. They outshouted our sin and upstaged our unworthiness.

The Author and Finisher of our faith extended the highest act of grace to have a relationship with people who don't deserve anything from him.

Too Convenient a View of Salvation

Many Christians prefer to talk about the cross in a generic way that inclines us to view Jesus' death as a sacrificial act for the sins of the world rather than a personal intervention to rescue you and me from our own wretchedness. Sometimes I wonder if it's our inclination to assign God's love only to the run-of-the-mill infractions that makes us feel justified in punishing and rejecting our spouse when they really, *really* blow it.

But when Jesus was hanging on the cross for you and me, he was seeing us from the depths of his grace-filled love. He sees you this way even though . . .

- you can't stop clicking on those porn sites.
- you're jealous of your friend's success.
- you're lusting over—or having an affair with—a coworker.
- you hate your parents (or your spouse's parents) and secretly wish they would die.
- you were promiscuous in college but told your spouse you weren't.
- you're addicted to "mommy porn."

No matter how wrong or shameful your actions have been, Jesus died to love you beyond them. He did this because you are part of his bride, the church, and he wanted to give you the wedding gift you most needed in order to be united with him: forgiveness. And it's this very wedding gift that he wants you, in turn, to give to your spouse.

A convincing appeal for extending grace to our spouse sits well when we're talking about minor things—but when our spouse has committed a serious, shameful sin, we feel justified in making a bee-line for the divorce court.

Why are we so quick to deny grace to our spouse for things Jesus couldn't wait to extend grace to us for?

The Catch

Grace isn't blind. Nor is it without nerve endings. A call to a grace-filled marriage doesn't mean we ignore, trivialize, or excuse our spouse's unacceptable behavior. Grace doesn't mean we lose our voice when it comes to dealing head-on with things that are clearly out of line. And grace doesn't remove consequences. God's grace is offered to us, but it isn't realized if we're unwilling to receive it properly. We have to repent. And our repentance must be more than an "Oh, excuse me, Lord. I'm sorry." It requires us to own our actions and refuse to continue in our self-destructive ways.

The example we get from God teaches us that when things aren't going well—or worse, when the wheels completely fall off our relationship—we need to race toward grace when it comes to how we respond.

Grace is not our default mode. It's contrary to our hardwiring. But there are two things we need to know. First, the Holy Spirit can give us the power to flip off the switch of our self-protective mode regardless of how bad the circumstances get in our marriage. Second, although there's pain in choosing to exercise grace, there's far more pain, sorrow, and fallout when we choose not to.

Grace for the Greater Sin

"Jan, sit down . . . please. I need to tell you something. My office assistant wasn't forced into sex on a date. I know that's what she implied. And the way you've surrounded her with tenderness is beyond anyone's expectations. All the support you gave her during her pregnancy, getting her nursery set up, and then holding her hand through the delivery was you doing what you do best: sacrificially loving others.

"But that son she delivered, that baby boy you held close to you and comforted in his first minutes of life—well, you need to know something about his father. I know who he is. In fact, so do you. You sleep with him.

"Jan. That's my son. *I'm* his dad!"

As confessions go, this one is in a category of its own. Fessing up to denting your spouse's car, arriving late to pick up your daughter from ballet class, or getting carried away with the Visa card sounds like the music from your high school years next to the betrayal, humiliation, and insult that Phil subjected Jan to.

The woman who had given birth to Phil's son was a lady who helped Phil and Jan in their business endeavors. Phil and this woman had an affair right under Jan's nose. But because Jan had no reason to suspect, their liaisons went undetected until the baby was born. If you want to stab your marriage in the heart, just go out and give that part of your life you promised to reserve for your spouse to an out-sider and then concoct a lie to explain it away.

When you count the months building up to the affair, the pro-longed period that Phil carried on the affair, the countdown to the delivery, and the month or so that Jan helped care for this child, the actual time frame was a couple of years. Years of betrayal.

You can see how their story could have ended like most of these kinds of stories end: in the dissolution of their marriage and the de-mise of everyone's future potential, especially this innocent child.

Did I mention that Phil was in the ministry? He had other busi-ness endeavors, but his primary role was that of a minister. So here was a guy who was doctrinally sound but personally shallow. If you had been watching his life during this time, you wouldn't have seen any serious signal of what was happening between him and Jan. It was an imperceptible drift. The fact is, most events like these aren't the result of a blowout in the relationship but rather are the conse-quence of a slow leak in devotion over a prolonged period of time.

Jan was a gem of a lady who was encouraging and supportive of Phil's interest, yet she and Phil grew apart. There was nothing specific, no big fights; they just got busy and comfortable living parallel lives. In the process, Phil began to feel unappreciated. When he started hearing praise from his assistant at work, he realized that he enjoyed it. This scenario is the classic recipe for an affair. Down he went.

But there is absolutely no excuse for infidelity, and Phil would be the first to pound this point home. God convicted Phil of his sin. Conviction is the fever God gives us that tips us off to our greater spiritual infection and pushes us toward its only true cure: repen-tance. God's convicting grace put a headlock on Phil in order to rescue him from his foolishness, his floundering relationship with God, and his broken relationship with Jan.

When Phil came to grips with what he'd done—to the child, to this child's mother, and to Jan—he did the only thing a person can do who wants any good to come out of a situation like this: He humbly came before God in complete brokenness and asked for his forgiveness. He poured out his heart before God in confession, making no excuses, assuming full responsibility, and humbly prepared to bear the personal consequences of his sin.

Phil found forgiveness. It's the same forgiveness King David found when he, too, committed adultery. King David said, "Blessed is the one whose transgression is forgiven, whose sin is covered. . . . I acknowledged my sin to you, and I did not cover my iniquity; I said, 'I will confess my transgressions to the LORD,' and you forgave the iniquity of my sin" (Psalm 32:1, 5 ESV). As Phil put it, "Sinning against your spouse is a horrible thing, but the process of restoring a marriage must begin at the beginning . . . with your relationship with God."

Next, Phil had to come clean with Jan. Fortunately for him, he had married a woman who experienced and understood God's grace.

The Gritty Work of Grace

Phil and Jan live in a charming home that has several fireplaces. There's one fireplace that warms my heart every time I'm near it, and it doesn't need a fire in it to do the job. It was on the couches beside this fireplace where Phil made the appointment to meet with Jan and confess his enormous sin to her. It was at this same fireplace that Phil found grace waiting for him.

Of course Jan was shocked and devastated by the truth. She realized that their relationship wasn't what she thought it was. Their lives would be forever changed, and a child was going to be center stage. Jan felt the hurt, pain, and rawness of Phil's sin against her.

But she chose to respond with grace. It wasn't grace offered without pain. There were no naive, happily-ever-after assumptions attached to the grace she extended to Phil. Jan knew their marriage was in distress, and their lives, from this moment on, would be radically altered. She didn't presume that her willingness to forgive Phil would necessarily save their marriage. But she knew that the grace God had shown her over the years was the same grace she must offer to her husband. Because she chose to forgive, the ball was back in Phil's court regarding their future together.

His unconditional repentance laid the foundation for them to start to rebuild their marriage. It was far from easy. The year after the confession was a year of deep anguish, intense prayer, tested patience, and weathered perseverance. But repentance and grace framed the decisions that followed. As a couple, Phil and Jan made sure there was full confession. Phil owned all of his actions, took full responsibility, and made zero excuses. They read Scripture together and spent daily time with each other in prayer. They submitted themselves to the authority of Scripture and the counsel of godly, trustworthy friends. Phil's involvement in ministry was placed on hold, and the question of if or when he might once again be involved in church leadership was left in the hands of the godly leaders to whom he was submitting.

Obviously, Phil completely reconfigured his life. He willingly and enthusiastically submitted his schedule for Jan's approval. He severed emotional ties with the mother of his son, but both Phil and Jan made sure that the woman and her son were more than cared for through the proper channels. And they began the accountable steps necessary to enable Phil to play his proper role as a dad to this boy.

They took the advice Jesus gave to the church of Ephesus when they had "left" their "first love" (Revelation 2:4 NASB). Jesus gave three practical pieces of advice to follow to rekindle their love for him: "*Remember* from where you have fallen, and *repent* and *do* the things you did at first" (v. 5 NASB).

Phil and Jan remembered what it was like when their hearts were a team, they stopped doing the deeds that had pulled them apart, and they vowed to once again do the things that had brought them together in the first place. They uncluttered their schedules, started dating each other again, and took the vacation they had been putting off. They returned to thinking, deciding, and operating as a couple.

Jan realized she had some work to do in her own heart. For starters, she had to refuse to beat up on Phil by revisiting the hurt. If their marriage was going to heal, they had to leave his sin at the foot of the cross. She fought for her marriage through the power of God's mercy, faith, and love. She knew in due time, God would restore the years the locust had eaten (Joel 2:25). She renewed her commitment to being a godly helpmate.

Phil and Jan discovered a deeper love for each other by being not only recipients of God's grace but ambassadors of it as well. They found freedom in transparency, safety in vulnerability, and a new depth to their intimacy.

The Rest of the Story

At this writing, this incident in Phil and Jan's life took place almost twenty years ago. Two decades of rekindling, rebuilding, and restoring their marriage have created a love story that eclipses anything they had before their marital blowout. Their commitment to God, to each other, to their kids, to the child from the affair, and even to the mother of that boy is one of the greatest grace stories I've ever witnessed. If you went to their church, you'd see Phil and Jan, their children, their grandchildren, their new son, and that boy's mother all sitting in the same front row, worshipping God and learning God's truth *together*.

Most outsiders looking in would want to give all the credit to Jan, since so much of the outcome hinged upon her response. She'd correct you in a heartbeat. "No, no, no," she'd say. "What you're seeing here is the fruit of God's amazing grace poured out over people who didn't deserve anything from him. We couldn't have done this without grace."

Like Phil and Jan, we have choices in how we configure our marriage relationship. And I applaud all those who willingly and happily submit to the truth of Scripture regarding purposes, roles, and goals as a couple. But without the Grace Lens, the best couples out there will quickly run out of the stuff they need to keep their hearts close. Jesus was filled with truth *and* grace (John 1:14). People like Phil and Jan could articulate the truth part of the story all day long, but their marriage couldn't thrive until they invited God to allow his grace to define the context in which they lived out that truth.

Grace-filled marriages keep the application of forgiveness up and running in couples' lives. It's always on, always there, always ready to be applied . . . for those minor disappointments that go with the territory and for those full-scale hits to the heart that only God's grace can overcome.

Getting Practical

Up to this point, we've looked at the *philosophical* priority of God's grace as the context framing our relationship with our spouse. We saw that grace is the divine lens God maintains when he deals with us, so why don't we do the same? We encouraged you to let God's grace be the lens through which you view your spouse, whether at their best or worst. The idea is to let God's gracious perspective define every aspect of your relationship.

In the rest of this book, we will see what a grace-filled marriage looks like. I'll show you how you can live out God's grace in the daily ins and outs/ups and downs of your marriage. But this next part needs a quick setup. If you'll lend me your imagination, we can do this fairly efficiently.

Suppose an emissary from heaven shows up at your wedding reception, pulls you aside, and says, "For you two to have the kind of relationship that brings out the best in each other and maximizes your potential as a couple, you'll need a *strategic* plan that covers all the demands you're going to face as a married couple. Do you know what that plan looks like?"

You probably say, "I haven't a clue what you're talking about. I mean, we love each other, and we want to be nice to each other. Is that what you're talking about?"

The emissary smiles and says, "No. *Love* and *nice* are fine features of your relationship, of course, but they won't get you through the tough stuff. I'm talking about a strategy that will serve you well even when life is working after hours to tear your loving and nice hearts apart."

"I don't know what you're talking about," you say.

"No problem," he says. "That's why I'm here. Consider this a wedding gift from God himself. I'd like to give you a strategic plan for your love that is a direct extension of his relationship with his bride, the church."

"Okay, I'm listening. What have you got?"

He reaches into his coat pocket, pulls out a pen, grabs a cocktail napkin from the reception table where you're sitting, and says, "How about I make this simple? Here's a big-picture strategy for maintaining a heart connection with each other, no matter what life brings your way." Then he draws a house on that napkin and maps out the strategy within that drawing. It looks something like this:

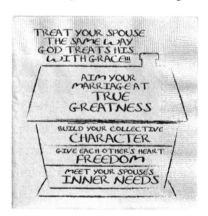

He's drawn out four dimensions of God's grace, four things God is always doing for you. You read what the emissary wrote. "Okay," you say. "I'm seeing the big picture, but could you be more specific?"

The emissary smiles. "I knew you'd ask that." So he flips over the napkin and says, "Let's put some relational targets on each level." This is what he draws for you:

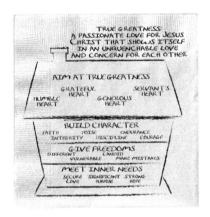

"If you make this strategy your gift to each other," he continues, "you're going to be way ahead of most couples leaving their wedding reception. But don't make the mistake of thinking this is a simple checklist. It's anything but. It's a guide that simply outlines for you the same things God is doing for his spouse, the church. This will only work if you carry it out in God's power.

"So the last piece of advice I'd like to give you is this: your relationship to each other will stand or fall primarily on your relationship with Christ. The closer each of you pulls your heart to him, the more natural this strategic plan is going to be. So love God first and love God most, and these things will be logical extensions of that relationship."

With that, he picks up the napkin, hands it to you, and says, "Don't be afraid. For the Lord your God is with you two wherever you go and whatever you encounter along the way."

With this strategy before us, let's spend the rest of our time learning exactly how you can meet your spouse's inner needs, set your spouse's heart free, build your character as a couple, and aim your marriage at a future of true greatness . . . all in the power of God's grace.

—

PART 2

—

WHAT DOES GRACE LOOK LIKE
IN A MARRIAGE?

CHAPTER 4

Grace Gives You a Secure Love

—

"That guy really creeps me out."

Darcy seldom voices criticism about people. She tends to notice the good in folks. If she has a concern about someone, she usually does her best to look beyond it. So when Darcy broke the silence on our drive home from a dinner party with this observation about our host, I assumed there was something major pushing her to break from her standard operating procedure.

We had been invited to a small gathering hosted by a couple that enjoyed celebrity status in our church circle. He was a gifted communicator who was popular with the youth crowd. His high-level commitment to fitness and good looks made him come across as one of the kids even though he was old enough to be their father. He had even written a couple of spiritually focused books geared to young people. One thing I knew about him: he had more talent in his pinkie than I had in my whole body.

I had spent most of the evening on the patio with the men while our host and his wife had held court inside with the women. Though he and I had visited briefly, most of it was small talk.

When I inquired about Darcy's statement, I was reminded that

God gives many of us spouses with a sixth sense that protects us from dangers that could otherwise catch us off guard. She said she felt certain our host wasn't practicing what he taught. I reminded her that the line of people struggling with that problem would stretch around the globe . . . and she'd find me standing in it on occasion. But she wasn't talking about the standard struggles all people of faith wrestle with when it comes to living what we believe. She said, "This is way deeper than that." I asked her to elaborate, and she summarized her convictions in one sentence: "He treats his wife like she's a piece of trash."

She went on to tell how he flirted with two of the women at the dinner party. He was a storyteller, a life-of-the-party type of guy, yet he often described the physical features of the women in his stories. He dropped in words like *fit*, *thin*, and *well built* though this information had nothing to do with the point he was making. He did this while his wife was standing next to him. What brought Darcy's blood to a rolling boil was the fact that his wife was struggling to meet the physical standards her husband idolized in women. She had mentioned to Darcy how hard it had been to shed the weight she put on as a result of childbirth. This explained why Darcy had spent most of the evening trying to ignore our host while sticking by the side of our hostess. It also explains why she wanted to leave as soon as was socially acceptable.

One of the reasons we had been invited was that this man was working on a ministry project and wanted to enlist me in what he was doing. Darcy said, "His life is a contradiction, and their marriage is a train wreck waiting to happen. If I were you, I'd stay as far away from him and his ministry project as you can."

I took her advice.

Unfortunately, she turned out to be right. In these situations, we long for our instincts to be wrong. Neither of us desires a downfall for anyone. Yet certain laws of love cannot be broken if we want love to thrive. If we break those laws—especially over and over without remorse—we shouldn't be surprised when love dies.

Years later, the underbelly of this couple's flawed and graceless relationship was exposed, and they lost their marriage. Our hostess called on us to help her as she worked to rebuild her life after sexual scandal, public humiliation, and divorce. We were eager to give her all the help we could, but so much damage had been done. She was a mere emotional shadow of what she had been at her dinner party.

Our Inner Needs

We each marry people who have three driving inner needs. I'm not referring to physical needs like food, clothing, or shelter. Nor am I talking about health, education, and welfare needs, which have their place but don't carry the same power to rule the heart. I'm referring to the three needs that drive our passions, frame our self-view, and determine our capacity to maximize our closest relationships.

So what are these three inner needs? Let's use some alliteration to make them easier to remember:

Security
Significance
Strength

We're all driven by a need to know we're *secure*. We're all driven by a need to know we're *significant*—that we have intrinsic worth and value. And we're all driven by a need to know we have the *strength* required to face whatever life brings our way.

Think about this for a moment: Every child is born with these three needs. But infants possess no power to meet them on their own. That's where parents come in. When you consider the things a good parent does to care for an infant, you can categorize almost all of them under one or more of these inner needs. Likewise, when a parent doesn't meet a child's needs for security, significance, and strength—especially in the early years—this child goes into the future with voids that Satan is more than happy to fill with his knock-offs. That's why as parents we must be aware of what these needs are and be deliberate about consistently meeting them.[1]

When we get married, our spouse comes with the fuel gauges on each of these inner needs pointing toward "full" or "empty," based on how they were raised. In a grace-filled marriage, we make it our aim to use our words and actions to coax the gauges of our spouse's inner needs more and more into the "full" position.

Coaxing Each Other's Hearts toward Full

The host and hostess of the dinner party had hearts running on the mere fumes of security, significance, and strength. In fact, in spite of his role as a Christian speaker to young people, our host's three driving inner needs were dominated by the counterfeits the enemy had offered him—looks, applause, possessions, power, recognition, popularity, and control. He drank the Kool-Aid from the dark side, and regardless of how accurately he taught God's truth to young people, his refusal to let God's grace define him set him up to fall.

I'm sure we could look at this man's childhood and build a case for why he was the way he was, but none of that really matters, since he's an adult now. It might explain things, but it doesn't excuse anything. None of us can use an unfortunate upbringing as an alibi. It's time we take responsibility for our actions. Had our host done that, he might still have a front-row seat to God's majesty. Instead, he's a footnote.

But I've got good news! If you've put your faith in God's work for you on the cross through his Son, Jesus, he's all about transformation. He moved heaven and earth to empower us to put our old systems behind us and let God make everything about us new (2 Corinthians 5:17). Grace-filled marriages operate in constant awareness of each spouse's driving inner needs for security, significance, and strength— and both spouses consistently commit to meet these needs in each other . . . graciously.

A Secure Love

The primary way our heart feels secure is when we *know* we are loved. No doubts, no misgivings, no shadowlands where second-guessing and fear play games with our confidence. Among other things, Christ died for us so we can know once and for all that we are completely, ultimately, and profoundly loved.

Yet in the opening pages of Scripture, we see God make a man with a void that even God wasn't going to meet. He made a human, put him in the garden of Eden, and said, "It is not good for the man to be alone. I will make a helper suitable for him" (Genesis 2:18). God created marriage for lots of reasons, among them was so that we could have an intimate heart connection to someone with whom we could be naked and unashamed (v. 25).

So God made Eve, and then he performed a wedding. He decorated Eden for the ceremony, wrote the processional music for the heavenly instruments, and rehearsed the angelic choir to serenade the couple. Like a father with his daughter on his arm, God brought Eve to Adam and offered him the chance of a lifetime—to team with someone who was bone of his bone and flesh of his flesh as he took on life (v. 23). In his wedding homily, God framed marriage as an arrangement where we commit to leave our parents, cling to each other, and "become one flesh" (v. 24). He urged Adam and Eve to be fruitful, multiply, and steward all that God had entrusted to them (1:28).

Many people assume the word *fruitful* refers to having kids. But limiting this word to having kids is missing the bigger point. If we throw out some synonyms, I think we'll better see what God was challenging them to do. *Fruitful* is *abundant, successful, productive, rewarding*. This refers to far more than simply replacing ourselves. God is talking about creating a culture *as a couple* where our emotional, intellectual, and spiritual potential is maximized by being a twosome in ways it never could be if we fly solo.

So how are you doing in that department? Is your marriage making you better or bitter? Is it drawing you closer or driving you apart? Is it making it easier for you to live for God or complicating things? You can move in the right direction simply by doing for your spouse what God does for his: make it your aim, through the power of his grace, to build a *secure* love into your spouse through the careful words you use and the deliberate actions you take.

Nailing Down Love

Early in our marriage, Darcy and I realized it would be a lot easier to love each other if we clarified exactly what is assumed in the word *love*.

We needed direction because we came into our marriage fairly self-focused and full of our own agendas. We needed something succinct, concise, and unwavering to frame our thinking and actions. When a verb like *love* is applied broadly and flippantly—"I love you, and I really love this beef jerky"—it loses much of its precious and potent edge.

We are called to raise our spouse's sense of security by loving them in a way that causes them to grow more confident about how dearly they are loved by us. A secure love makes it much easier to give and receive grace.

So Darcy and I came up with a definition of *love* that has proven to thrive under fire:

> *Love is the commitment of my will to your needs*
> *and best interests, regardless of the cost.*

This definition is a direct extension of God's love for us. He committed his divine will to our needs and best interests at the most extreme price in eternity. And he didn't aim his love at us because of our goodness or our noble behavior. Scripture says, "God demonstrates his own love for us in this: While we were still sinners, Christ died for us" (Romans 5:8). God directed his love toward us because of what he sees in us as people made in his image.

We raise our spouse's sense of security by committing to their needs and best interests, regardless of the price tag for us. We put our ego, time, personal preferences, and conveniences up for grabs for the sake of loving our spouse securely.

"Needs and best interests" address the emotional, intellectual, and spiritual aspects of love that should be fairly obvious. But these words also include the hard side of love. Sometimes the love we need to give our spouse is tough and gritty. There's nothing loving about watching a spouse carry on self-destructive behavior and doing nothing. Thus, a secure love requires us to step up and do what's in our spouse's best interests, even when they don't think it is (like intervening in an alcoholic's life). But most of the time, this definition of love serves itself up like a fresh cappuccino to the heart.

Our Spouse Feels Secure When We Accept Them

We feel insecure when our spouse refuses to accept the things about us that are simply us. I'm not talking about weaknesses that can stand improvement. Nor am I talking about bad habits or unacceptable behavior. I'm talking about the things about us that aren't right or wrong but just *are*. They're our personality quirks, mannerisms, physical abilities, and body types . . . to name a few. They're the things that make each of us one of a kind.

One week before I got married, I bought a "muscle car." My brother Tom and I spent a day and a half up in Pennsylvania rebuilding the engine. A few days before the big day, I showed up in Annapolis, Maryland, ready to ride off into the future with Darcy. For the gearheads reading this, it was a '66 Pontiac GTO. It was far from new, but Tom and I got it running like it was. I thought Darcy would love driving it. I was wrong. She complained about the way it tended to peel a bit of tire off every time she popped the clutch going from first to second, and sometimes even into third. That's why I bought it! I tried to explain to her how cool that was and how hot she looked doing it. She was not impressed. She wanted something tame, manageable, and quiet. Within a year, I sold the GTO and bought a Volkswagen! It was one of my first major disappointments in my marriage.

Had I been quicker on the uptake, I would have seen the car as a metaphor of a bigger reality. I had married a woman who was cautious by nature. She preferred to know where we were going before we took off, and she liked to have some say on the route we'd choose (read: the one with the least unknowns). Darcy was a woman of forethought and deliberateness. And she didn't feel comfortable when she was put in charge of something that left her at the mercy of things she couldn't control. So you're thinking, *If that's true, why'd she marry you?*

Good point. I was a bona fide risk taker. I preferred pushing the envelope in fourth gear. Road maps were for amateurs. When Darcy and I found ourselves sitting across the table from each other every night and waking up under the same blankets every morning, our preferences started to grate on each other. But even though my "Let's see what's down that dark back road through the woods" attitude often made Darcy nervous, she knew that was one of the things that attracted her to me. She was careful in how she lived out her day-to-day life, but she wanted to harness her heart and her future to someone who wasn't intimidated by unknowns or rattled by foiled plans.

In the same way, I was drawn to Darcy because she was careful and calculated. I knew that for me to succeed, I'd need someone who could keep my feet on the ground and help me put planning and organization around my dreams. I also needed someone who was invested enough in me to get in my face every once in a while and tell me when I was being an idiot. Thus, the fetching Mrs. Kimmel.

Too bad that wasn't the position we defaulted to. For the first few years, instead of graciously honoring each other's hardwiring and accepting how our differences could help us operate as a team, Darcy and I marginalized each other's preferences and mocked each other's strengths. She considered me reckless, and I considered her somewhat embalmed. With each barb, our security fuel gauges moved toward empty.

I've seen couples miss the chance to refuel each other's sense of security by carping about physical issues that aren't in that person's control. Criticism about our spouse's body type drains their sense of security almost every time. Here's a note you might want to make to yourself: your spouse's DNA tends to confine their options when they stand in front of the full-length mirror. Most of what you see is genetics—part of the wonderful artwork God chose for your spouse's body. But if you criticize physical features over which your spouse has little to no control, it will be hard for them to feel a secure love.

Comparison doesn't help a spouse feel secure either. In grad school, Darcy and I socialized with one of my classmates and his wife. At first we thought our friendship would be a good fit, but it was obvious his wife wasn't impressed with her husband's chosen profession of vocational ministry. Since I was heading down that same road, I assumed she wasn't impressed with me either. Fortunately, I didn't have to live with her. Unfortunately, he did. She compared him to friends who had chosen career paths she felt were more prestigious. His confidence as a man shrank with each comparison. But his confidence as a husband paid the biggest price. She didn't respect his calling. She didn't appreciate what she assumed would be limited earning power. She didn't like the subordinating their life often took to other people's needs. Not surprisingly, he only lasted a couple of years as a pastor.

Even though he left the ministry, the comparisons continued. I could have told him that. The problem wasn't his vocation or earning power; it was her lack of grace. His wife refused to extend to him the grace that a loving person does to bring out the best in their spouse. This guy had all the stuff to be something great for God. The only one who couldn't see this reality was his wife. Her lack of grace for the man he was deep down inside shriveled his sense of security to nothing. No acceptance—no security.

Meanwhile, Darcy and I figured out we were working against each other's hearts. We weren't showing each other much grace when it came to how God had configured us. We were also disrespecting him in the process. He made us with our unique personalities. He drew us together to help fill each other's gaps. God could make us much more as a couple than we could ever be as individuals. Once we started seeing each other through the Grace Lens and allowing God's grace to frame our words and actions toward each other, a wonderful chain reaction started taking place. I started appreciating and applauding her carefulness. She, in turn, started applauding and appreciating my daring and dreaming. God's grace helped us develop an attitude that asked, "How do I make it easier for my spouse to do what they do best?" This maximized our potential and capacity as a couple. Our willingness to infuse our relationship with grace as we accepted each other brought more laughter, calm, peace, passion, and confidence into our marriage.

And there was another benefit of this decision to accept each other: it helped us mature beyond the downsides of our personalities. Over the years, Darcy has grown into much more of a risk taker. She now suggests the scenic route over the sure thing, the backstreets of emotions over the thoroughfare. And I've learned the wisdom in planning, risk factoring, and proceeding carefully. I still love driving in fourth gear and close to the edge of the road of life, but I prefer to keep my emotional, spiritual, and intellectual GPS lit up along the way.

Our love grows far more secure when we *accept* the things about our spouses that make them who they are. How are you doing in this area? Do you see your spouse's uniqueness and strengths as something to be marginalized or applauded?

Our Spouse Feels Secure When We Have a Strong Affiliation with Their Heart

Darcy and I met a couple in the Northwest who appeared to place a high priority on their marriage. They headed up a local committee that sponsored a marriage conference every year. Both were charming and skilled at what they did. When we showed up to speak at their event, it was well attended. This couple worked all weekend to make sure everything ran smoothly—behind the scenes but never side by side—among the attendees learning how to grow their hearts closer to each other.

Big events usually have big details attached to them, so we didn't give it a second thought. But Darcy and I stayed connected to this couple through e-mails, occasional phone calls, and Christmas cards. That's when we came to see that these two were living not as a team but rather as roommates. If she had free time, she spent it with her friends or her children. Same with him. They had hobbies, but they weren't mutual hobbies. He liked to fish; she liked to do anything but fish. She referred to it as his "stupid" pastime . . . "that waste of time he calls 'fishing.'" He didn't speak well of the passions of her heart either. It was fine with them both. They each liked what they liked and could not care less about what fascinated their spouse. They thought this was normal. They went on separate vacations, too, taking along a friend rather than each other. You couldn't say they were living parallel lives, because that would assume they were at least heading in the same direction. They were living opposite lives.

Several years after we met them, Darcy and I once again crossed their path. Their lack of affiliation had taken its toll not only on them as a couple but on them as individuals. Fear about life in general and doubts about their faith in particular had turned them into ghosts of the people we originally met. When people are growing in the grace and knowledge of the Lord—especially as a couple—one of the ways this growth should be obvious is by the spike upward you notice in their personal confidence, their individual sense of purpose, and the muscle they exercise as a team. These two had gone backward. The most obvious evidence was how little they trusted each other. When you refuse to develop an affiliated heart with your spouse, you shouldn't be surprised that your love struggles with deep-seated insecurity.

Before I leave this point, let me mention a word you'll need if you want to build a secure love into your spouse. *Honor.* This word speaks of the high value you place on the other person. One of the ways you value your spouse is by being interested in the things that interest them. You notice. You care. Honor is also about empathy. When you honor your spouse, you value your spouse so much that you can't contain the "woo-hoos!" on their behalf in victory and you likewise hurt deeply with them in defeat.

All these aspects of enabling your spouse to feel a secure love come from a heart of grace. One of the greatest *grace* chapters in the Bible is Romans 12. If any passage describes what grace looks like covered in sweat and tears, it's this one: "Be happy with those who are happy, and weep with those who weep. Live in harmony with each other. Don't be too proud to enjoy the company of ordinary people. And don't think you know it all!" (vv. 15–16 NLT).

This couple we got to know in the Northwest had gone the opposite direction. No shared interests; no shared honor. They missed out on having a grace-filled marriage because they didn't stay closely affiliated as a team in order to build a secure love.

Our Spouse Feels Secure When We Show Them Consistent Affection

Our hearts respond well to regular and generous helpings of affection. That's because love grows much more secure when our spouse is lavish about giving and receiving meaningful touch.

Before I address the obvious issue of skin-to-skin affection, I need to acknowledge nontouch forms of affection—like filling up your wife's car without being asked, making coffee for her when you get up every morning, and keeping quiet about how many pairs of shoes she owns. Or how about smiling when your husband wears his favorite shirt or boots over and over again and believes in both redundancy and mutually assured destruction when it comes to his tool collection? Then there are love notes, love texts, love e-mails. The options for nontouch affection are endless. To *affect* our spouse is simply to do something to them or for them that warms their emotions and inclines them to feel a more secure sense of love from us.

Which brings us back to skin. God built a network of nerve endings all over us, and he tripled down in our sex organs. Without debate, the greatest context for the expression and reception of affection is marriage. A tender touch can profoundly change the way a spouse views life. But it's not limited to that. Grace-filled, generous affection affects everything about us—how we view ourselves, our spouse, our marriage, our purposes as a couple, even our attitude toward God.

When I was in grad school, I worked at Baylor hospital. Part of my job was to help pathologists perform autopsies. There's something I've always believed but could never prove—namely, that the nerve endings that bring comfort, relaxation, joy, or pleasure are wired directly to our soul. Because the pathologists and I couldn't pin down the exact location of a person's soul, I couldn't convince the good doctors of the connection. Physical proof or not, it's true. God made us to respond at the core of our being to tender touch, meaningful touch, sensual touch.

Guys, have you ever had an itch on your back that you can't reach? You're ready to rub against the side mirror on your truck when your wife steps beside you, slips her hand under your shirt, and starts moving her long nails up and down your spine. Who needs a mirror? Who even wants a mirror? I suddenly hate mirrors. Let's hear it for sensitive wives and long fingernails!

Ladies, let's say you're trying to put on a necklace, but between the microscopic clasp, your hand lotion, and your nails, you simply can't get it to cooperate. Then your husband comes along and, without being asked, says, "Let me help." He drapes the necklace around your neck, sets the clasp, and then drops his hands down to your shoulders, places a kiss on your neck, and says, "You look wonderful."

The fact is, physical affection is a powerful agent for building secure love into our spouse. Holding hands, hugging, and kissing all add layer upon layer of security in the love within each other's hearts. But these are all warm preliminaries compared to the ultimate display of affection in marriage—sex.

Grace-Filled Sex

What does grace have to do with sex? Everything. If anything, our sexual relationship is the litmus test on how serious we are about being an agent of God's grace when it comes to our spouse.

For a lot of couples, if you want to get them to laugh, just bring up their sex lives. For these same couples, if you want to get them to cry, just bring up their sex lives. It's tragic that for too many married couples, the thing they most looked forward to enjoying *with God's blessing* in their relationship ends up being the dimension of their marriage that brings them the greatest disappointment.

It wasn't supposed to be this way. And perhaps for you, it isn't. You and your spouse may enjoy a robust, creative, and deeply satisfying sexual relationship. Good for you! But you're the exception. If the statistics are accurate and counseling clinics are to be believed, too many couples lose joy when it comes to the sexual dimension of their marriage.

Even bringing the subject up in a sermon, a marriage conference, or a book causes many couples to become defensive. I don't blame you if you're starting to do that right now. Sex has been an abused and confused part of our human relationships. Our culture trivializes it, Hollywood panders to it, pornographers capitalize on it, some Christian circles marginalize it, and too many couples worship it. Between the misleading of some and the failure to lead of others, it's not surprising that many couples who married to have the freedom to sexually express themselves under the banner of God's blessing soon feel utterly let down.

Although there are a lot of wonderful add-ons to our relationship as married couples (such as traveling, pursuing mutual interests, and merging our wits and resources), none of these, from a biblical point of view, require a marriage license. The unique thing—the set-apart thing—the Bible assigns to married couples is their freedom to enjoy each other sexually with God's blessing. Sex is that singular thing that makes you a married couple as opposed to just good friends. All the other features of your relationship can be shared with others (friendship, business interests, common causes), but sex is the one thing about you as a couple that isn't to be shared with anyone else.

Why is this arrangement even necessary? Because God made us sexual beings. He gave us sex to guarantee our continuation as a people. He threw a pleasure dimension into it to make sure people would be inclined to procreate. But he also wrapped sex up in the intricacies of love with the idea that it be confined to a married couple so that children would have the best possible context for their protection and a solid launch when they're ready to take on adulthood.

But that's not the total picture on sex. Not by a long shot. God made sex for our mutual pleasure and joy. He created it so that we can enjoy our built-in need and desire for sexual satisfaction in an obedient biblical context as well as the safety of a committed love relationship. He gave us a yearning for sex, and a grace-filled relationship moves that yearning to a focused object of it—the spouse we married.

Do you want to hear something wild? Do you remember when we discussed Adam and Eve earlier in this chapter? What this first couple had going for them that no couple has had since is the fact that they lived in an environment where there was no sin, no guilt, and no shame. Obviously, they figured out how to wreck all of that, but when Adam and Eve first became a couple, that's the kind of climate their love enjoyed. The last point made in the creation account is that they were "both naked, and they felt no shame" (Genesis 2:25). The next thing you read is the snake tempting Adam and Eve, and them blowing their great opportunity. But there's something I think we miss about God's gift of sex in marriage. To a certain degree (not completely, I realize), God gives us a taste of what Eden was like before sin entered the world when we experience sex in our marriage. He lets us be naked and unashamed with this person we've committed our vows and our life to.

Satan has, in the majority of cases, gained the upper hand when it comes to sex. He has polluted culture's view of sex so much so that even Christians fail to see God's design for sex—not just as a way that he uniquely joins the hearts of a man and a woman, but also as a way he blesses us. Instead of seeing sex as a gift from God meant to be enjoyed within marriage, we are deceived into viewing it as an appetizer to marriage and a bargaining chip once the vows are exchanged. God meant sex to be a high priority in marriage as a husband and wife enjoy and mutually satisfy each other. Unfortunately, between the distortions of the dark side and our selfishness, we often throw a wet blanket over something God meant to be a powerful source of delight and heart connection in our love together as couples.

The Antithesis of Grace-Filled Sex

In marriages that lack grace, couples can selfishly use sex in ways it was never meant to be applied. Let me list some common ways couples abuse each other and contradict their covenant before God in their sexual relationship.

1. Some use sex to manipulate something they want from their spouse. A lot of guys would say, "I don't care. At least she's having sex with me!" But over a long enough period of time, this selfish use of sex can turn a spouse's heart cold. It's not sex because your spouse wants you; it's sex because they want something else from you that you might not otherwise be inclined to give.

2. Some use sex as a reward. This turns a partner into a dog-and-pony show. "Roll over." "Sit." "Beg." "Good dog. Okay, I'll give you a treat now." That's all it is when you boil down this kind of intimacy. This graceless attitude toward sex doesn't build a secure love. It builds a jump-through-the-hoops love. It's a form of high control. This abuse of sex says, "I'll give you what you need from me if I think you deserve it. Otherwise, forget it." Is that how God treats you?

3. Some use sex as punishment. They withhold sex when they're angry at their spouse or want to make their spouse suffer for their misdeeds. These misdeeds can be subjective, arbitrary, and sometimes trivial. But does God withhold the blessings of our human needs (water, food, clothing, and shelter) to remind us of what misfits we are? Marriage is the only God-ordained outlet for meeting this unique human need.

4. Some see sex as an obligation rather than an opportunity to extend grace as well as bless their spouse. They may cooperate, accommodate, and even "perform" well. But because sex is not just Pilates with a jolt but an intricate weaving of bodies, souls, and spirits, it doesn't take long for the person on the receiving end of this obligatory sex to feel devalued.

Let me add two other ways that couples without grace default on the covenant they made before God to meet each other's needs.

Demanding sex. Sex is a physical gift that is to be offered *to* our spouse, not taken *from* our spouse. Demanding sex has nothing to do with the heart of God. Think of all the legitimate expectations that go with a healthy relationship with God: being generous to the poor, forgiving one another, exercising your spiritual gifts, serving the people around you . . . Which of these does God demand that we do? None. He makes it clear what devotion and commitment look like. But he leaves it to us to step forward and offer it back to him. Grace-filled couples treat each other the way God treats his bride. Our spouse cannot feel a secure love if we demand that they give us sex.

Defrauding sex. This is different from withholding sex as punishment, which we discussed earlier. And it could easily be seen as the logical response to someone who demands sex. But that's not the typical way this shows up in a marriage. Defrauding sex is when one spouse says, "I just don't want to for now . . . maybe indefinitely." This is another example of marital cruelty. Over the years I have counseled lots of couples who have huge heartbreak in the area of sex. Often I'll hear a spouse say, "Sex just doesn't do anything for me. I'm not interested." My response is, "Then you should have thought of that before you got married!" Sex is the unique feature of you as a married couple! Your spouse cast their hopes, desires, and fidelity with you. What are they supposed to do? They have no other morally and biblically acceptable outlets. They have real human needs. They entrusted this part of their life to you. It's cruel to say to them, "Sorry, but this part of marriage is unimportant to me."

But don't take my word for it; listen to the apostle Paul. He spoke for God himself when he discussed the subject of grace-filled sex in marriage in 1 Corinthians 7:5: "Do not deprive each other of sexual relations, unless you both agree to refrain from sexual intimacy for a limited time so you can give yourselves more completely to prayer. Afterward, you should come together again so that Satan won't be able to tempt you because of your lack of self-control" (NLT).

I realize there are extenuating circumstances that may be fueling a spouse's disinterest in sex. It could be a low libido with physiological roots, such as aging. It could be some mental or physical preoccupation like a degree program, a prodigal child, ailing parents, or pregnancy. It could be radical changes in the physical aesthetics of a spouse—changes that make it very difficult for the indifferent spouse to stir up the inclination. It could be a life-altering illness or injury. If you are experiencing any of these or other situations in your marriage, I urge you to seek the medical and spiritual help you need.

Then, of course, sexual indifference could be due to sexual experiences before you were married. Most married people reading this book had sex before marriage. For some of you, it was a choice you made. It's ironic that the sexual revolution, which promised so much fun, pleasure, and freedom, causes so much bondage, shame, and indifference for people once they finally get married. But for some of you, sex was a choice someone else made for you against your will. The wounds hold you hostage to the crimes done against you. Sex is such a powerful bonding agent that when it's been mishandled or misapplied outside of God's stated design, there can be a lot of toxic residual impact in marriage.

I could write another book dealing with what to do in these situations. This isn't the place to go into depth, but we need to acknowledge the biblical reality. Whether your sexual struggles are the result of your poor choices or the crimes of others against you, God's grace extends the power and victory of his finished work on the cross to release you from the guilt, shame, hurt, and regret. Satan wants you to keep these past regrets as open wounds that fester. He wants to keep the crimes as fresh memories that define and debilitate you. A major step of obedience to God and a major act of grace to our spouse is when we let God turn our wounds into sacred scars, and crimes against us into ancient history. Satan will tell you that can't be done. You've got to decide once and for all who you're going to both trust and obey.

There's release in confession, repentance, and forgiveness. God wants the sexual dimension of your marriage to be a point of great joy and heart connection. It might require confessing wrong choices you made in the past, repenting of them, and asking God and your spouse for forgiveness. It might require handing the crimes done against you to God and letting him mete out justice toward the wrongdoers (Romans 12:17–21) so that you can move on with your life. There's nothing gracious about letting the forces of evil hold you hostage to crimes done against you. God wants to release you from their hold so you can enjoy a full and free sexual life with your spouse.

I realize there are enormous complexities that make one think that past sexual experiences are inescapable, but a statement like that would never come from the Holy Spirit. So perhaps even the thought of never being able to get beyond these things is just the dark side continuing to lie to you. I don't know about you, but the last person I want having any say in how I'm supposed to respond in these kinds of situations is the evil one who got me there in the first place.

Regardless of the reasons, a married person should see meeting their spouse's sexual needs as one of their primary ministries to that person. The reasons we've discussed may explain a spouse's lack of desire for sex in general or their spouse in particular, but if we're going to bring God's grace to this dilemma, then the indifferent spouse must be willing to do all they can to rectify the problem. Fortunately, God's grace is sufficient for victory.

A Word from Darcy

Sex isn't supposed to be a god we worship. It's a gift from God we've been given for blessing each other.

I wanted to share something I've observed in my experience as a woman. I have found that many women view their husband's sexual needs as merely physical and put them on the same level as their own need for sleep. So as a mom, if you can go without sleep, you think, *That big baby can go without sex.*

We need to understand that a man's need for sexual fulfillment with his wife is more than just a physical need. It is comparable to our need as women to feel loved and accepted. What if we needed to spend time with our husband, desperately longed for some attention from him, or hadn't heard him tell us he loved us for a while and brought it up to him? How would we feel if he said he was too busy, too tired, or not in the mood to respond to these needs? Chances are we would be crushed. We must remember that our husband feels the same way when we shun his sexual needs. For most of our husbands, there is no greater way for them to feel love and acceptance from us than sexual fulfillment. This is a need God has put in them that he asks us to fulfill to the best of our ability.

Several years ago, Tim and I were speakers at several big arena events focusing on marriage. Somehow in God's cosmic humor, he chose us to stand up in front of thousands of people and speak about the subject of sex.

When you spend forty-five minutes talking about this intimate subject, people feel like they know you and can share all sorts of personal details with you. So I usually made myself scarce after our talk until we could escape to the airport. But I didn't realize that some people fly in to attend these events. So there we were at the airport one Saturday evening after speaking. Tim had gone to buy us something to eat when a man approached me with a big smile on his face and shook my hand. In what seemed like a very loud voice, he thanked me for our frank and fun discussion on sex. I wanted to become invisible. Then to emphasize how important this subject is to most men, he said, "You know, Darcy, men think about sex as often as women think about their kids. And how often is that? Well, constantly, if they're with their kids, and most of the time when they are not with their kids. You might want to pass that on to the ladies."

I thanked this man and then quickly went to find Tim. But what he said has stuck with me and helped me to realize that God has placed a unique need in our husbands that he has given wives the privilege to fulfill. In a grace-filled marriage, we love our spouse enough to set aside our agendas and make ourselves available to meet each other's needs. This type of commitment builds a secure love in their hearts. And this is a two-way street. The husband isn't the only one with sexual needs.

Grace-filled intimacy is about giving with enthusiasm and receiving with joy. The more we align our hearts with God's heart of grace, the more we can see the strategic role we play as an intimate partner with our spouse. God meant for our marriage bed to be a place of passion, joy, fun, adventure, and mutual satisfaction. And when the intimacy we enjoy there is an extension of our gracious desire to meet each other's needs, our love grows secure.

When we got married, Tim and I made a commitment to each other that we would maintain a "convenience-store attitude" toward each other's need and desire for sex. Convenience store? You know, those markets on the corner that are open 24 hours a day, 7 days a week, 365 days a year. And our observation over the decades of involvement in married couples' lives is that this is one of the key features of those who view each other through the Grace Lens. They appreciate their spouse's desire for them. They consider it a compliment. They desire the best for their mate. They take delight in being wanted and needed for such a precious part of their spouse's life—and they meet that need by participating enthusiastically.

This is the kind of commitment two grace-filled people make in a marriage. Please note: there's no room for a sex addict's diet—it's not gracious. There's no room in this system for the manipulator, demander, punisher, dog-and-pony-show rewarder, or the spouse who just shows up out of obligation. These attitudes don't pass the grace test.

Therefore, *no one* reading this could use it as material to coerce, guilt, or shame their spouse into alignment. That wouldn't be *grace-filled*! A proper response would be to ask God to give you the right attitude toward your spouse regarding your intimate life and leave any adjustments that need to be made to your spouse's attitude to the work of the Holy Spirit.

Obviously, even with our 24/7/365 commitment to each other, the Grace Lens helps us factor in the obvious parentheses: sickness, exhaustion, the demands and distractions of parenting, injury, pregnancy and its aftermath, preoccupations (finals, finishing degree programs, sick parents, caregiving responsibilities). Sexual needs go through seasons too. But the key is focusing outward toward the needs of your spouse regardless of what season you may be experiencing. Couples who make this gracious commitment to each other not only build each other's sense of a secure love, but they also enjoy a closeness of body and spirit they don't have to share with anyone else. Oh, and one more thing: they don't go around sexually hungry. They get to thrive in the midst of a sexually polluted culture because both of them face it satisfied and contented. This attitude is a huge offset to the pull of pornography or other sexual temptations in a husband's or wife's life.

Road Trips

After Darcy and I were married eight years, my role in ministry changed from being based at one church to speaking to churches all over the country. I've handled thousands of boarding passes, slept in many hotel rooms, and said, "Table for one" to many hostesses. I'm not complaining. I love what God has given me the privilege to do over the years.

When I travel somewhere, I'm usually the only speaker. Every once in a while, however, I participate in an event that has many speakers on the docket. Several years ago I was at one of these venues, and after everything was over, a couple of the other speakers and I went out to dinner. These were guys whom I knew by reputation but hadn't spent much time with. As the dinner conversation progressed, each guy started talking about his disappointing relationship with his wife. I just ate and listened. They were talking more to each other than to me, and in their discussion, they volunteered how marginal their sexual relationship was with their wives. The subject changed a couple of times. Dessert was ordered. Then one of the guys mentioned a time when a woman came on very strongly to him on one of his road trips. The other guy came back with a similar incident. Then they proceeded to recall one time after another when they found themselves face-to-face with easy opportunities to gain on the road what they weren't getting at home.

I thought about their conversation on my flight home, and after we got the kids to bed, I told Darcy about the challenges these guys had. I wasn't passing it on to disparage them but to make an observation about myself. I said to her, "I must have 'Complete Loser' written across my forehead, because in all of my travels, I've never had a woman come on to me. I must be the biggest dope on the speaking circuit."

She smiled and shook her head. Then she said, "No. That has nothing to do with it. You have your red light on. Those guys probably have their green lights on. Or, to give them the benefit of the doubt, perhaps yellow lights. Regardless, their struggles at home might have been communicating a message to those women. Women can tell when a man is sexually needy."

If I've had a red light on when it comes to other women all these years, it has nothing to do with me personally. I'm just as capable as any other person to make dumb choices in this area. Most likely my victory has more to do with God's grace in our marriage. This grace has helped Darcy and me see each other as gifts rather than projects, privileges rather than obligations. Our 24/7/365 availability to each other makes sure that neither of us is sexually hungry.

More couples than you think have figured this out. But if you're not one of them, don't panic . . . and don't give up. The God who bought and paid for you on a cross wants to give your marriage abundant life. He's ready to empower you to happily *accept* each other as glorious one-of-a-kinds. He's excited to enfold your hearts with a sense of *affiliation* like you've never known. And he's eager to implant an earnest *affection* for each other into your hearts that will give you both a new tenderness and passion for each other.

This is how God's grace builds a secure love through a grace-filled marriage. It's available to any and all of us who have placed our faith in him. He went before us to show us what a grace-filled love looks like. And if you want to know what to do to make this yours, just treat your spouse the way Jesus treats his.

———

CHAPTER 5

Grace Gives You a Significant Purpose

———

We want to matter. We *need* to matter. We were created to matter.

When we have a deep sense that our life makes a difference, our capacity to love and be loved can move into the ionosphere. Take away our sense of intrinsic worth, and awful things—sometimes dangerous things—happen to us and others. Especially in marriage. A sense of insignificance can make us needy, dissatisfied, nagging, jealous, and bitter. That's why the grace to help your spouse sense a significant purpose will draw your hearts closer.

Maybe if we understood this more as married couples, we'd spend more time smiling at life and at each other. If we made it our aim to use our words and actions to help our spouse add another layer to their inner sense of significance, we'd be doing more than smiling; we'd be doing the happy dance most of the time.

Obviously, life knows how to sucker punch everyone, and we all get our turn. But even in those times when there's nothing to be happy about, a grace-filled commitment to meet each other's need for significance enables us to navigate our way through life's downturns. And in the process of weathering life together in a significant way, our value as a couple will go up and up.

We could all take a lesson from the wedding rings we wear.

It's not a coincidence that the symbols chosen for a wedding happen to be two of the most valuable items on the globe. Gold and diamonds have a lot in common, although they're about as different as two things could be. It takes many years and a lot of intense pressure to even get them to the point where they're worth the effort to pursue. That pursuit involves mining—a pricey and dicey endeavor that requires a heavy human commitment. In their natural state, neither gold nor diamonds look like something you'd consider precious. To the untrained eye, they are little more than a bucket of rocks—ordinary, certainly nothing *valuable*. That's where the refining process takes over with its heating, cooling, tooling, and polishing. Once gold and diamonds are prepared individually, they have a *forever* quality about them. But when you put them *together* in a setting, something even better happens. They make each other more valuable than they were as a stand-alone diamond or piece of refined gold. That's because together, they're a work of art.

Does this process sound familiar? Maybe gold and diamonds won the nod for sealing the vows of a marriage for more reasons than their value.

Speaking of works of art, when Darcy and I married, we weren't in the same league as a masterpiece hanging in some high-end art gallery. That's because you have to average the two of us together to come up with a common artistic value. She, of course, was already a magnum opus in my book, while I was struggling to hold on to my paint-by-numbers status. That's not false humility or self-deprecating. I believed I had potential and so did she, but at that point in my young journey through life, my potential was more sketchbook quality than canvas ready.

It was during the Christmas break of my final year of college that I decided to see if Darcy would be open to the idea of taking on life with me . . . until death us do part. This required a ring, which in turn required money. At the time, I was a poor college student. And I was born with a plastic spoon in my mouth, so there weren't any trust funds to raid. I did what I could with what I had to work with at the time. When I walked out of the jewelry store with that little box in my pocket, it held the sum total of just about every penny I had. I knew it would never come close to complementing the finger of the woman who would wear it. But if she chose to put it on, it would at least symbolize what we'd want our love and our relationship as a couple to represent—something precious and timeless, something that would make each of us worth more as a duet than we could ever pull off as solo acts. But more than that, it would make us more valuable as a couple to the world around us.

Marriage Potential

The diamond that marks our engagement and the gold rings that seal our vows signify what we're trying to become rather than what we are when we're standing in front of those witnesses. It doesn't matter how great of a show we staged for our wedding. The fresh flowers, rented suits, and white dress may present well in the wedding photos, but we can't Photoshop what's going to happen after they sweep up the rice. Happily ever after is how fairy tales end, not how marriages begin. The process of turning a couple into a masterpiece has more in common with the refining process it took to make the wedding rings we wear.

Which brings us back to our discussion on our three driving

inner needs. We marry people who have a need for security, significance, and strength. In the previous chapter we learned that the best way to meet our spouse's need for security is to build a secure love into their heart. Our spouse senses a secure love when they know they're *accepted* by us, when they enjoy a close *affiliation* to us, and when we give them regular and generous helpings of *affection*. In this chapter, we will look at how to meet our spouse's sense of significance.

Grace's Gift of Significance

When the Me Lens, Love If Lens, or Pious Lens slips between us and our spouse, it's next to impossible to meet their need to feel significant. The Grace Lens, however, sees beyond their shortcomings to their intrinsic value. That's because with God's grace-filled perspective, we're empowered to notice the contribution our spouse is making and the potential they have yet to realize—you know, the same way God sees us. Darcy and I learned this early in our marriage.

One week and two days after we got married, I attended orientation for incoming students to the master's in theology degree program at Dallas Theological Seminary. In those nine days leading up to this moment, I had fulfilled the primary goal I had going into my wedding, which was figuring how to get Darcy out of that dress she was wearing. We had also driven across seven states, moved into an old Victorian house in Dallas, and gone to church. Up to that point, I thought I was playing my cards quite well.

I wasn't feeling that way when I got home from orientation.

We both remember the conversation. It was one of those early hikes into transparency that most men prefer to avoid. At dinner that night I wasn't my normal effervescent self. Darcy sensed things didn't go the way I had hoped at orientation, so she asked what was bothering me. I responded with an evasive, "Nothing." She didn't budge. Which is how I ended up telling her what had taken the dance out of my day.

"Darcy, something went very wrong in the admissions department. I don't belong at this school. I'm in way over my head. You won't believe the people I met today. That room was filled with hundreds of 'who's who' types. There were people from Harvard, Yale, Cornell, and Stanford. There were high-ranking guys from the military and people who have assisted some of the most famous names in Christian work. Some people there already oversee major ministries. And then there was me. The highlight of my résumé is that I've taught a second-grade Sunday school class. And listen, Darcy, this isn't some pity party to try to get your sympathy. I'm telling you the truth; I'm in way over my head."

It's interesting what comparison can do to a person. I've seen comparison cause people to turn down social invitations, say no to employment opportunities, and go into debt trying to compete with the lifestyles of folks who don't even know, or care, that they exist. Talk about a poison pill—few things have such a toxic impact on your sense of significance than when you look around and conclude you're outshined, outclassed, and outgunned. But this sense of inadequacy is often fueled by perception that has nothing to do with reality. There was a good chance that many of the people I'd felt eclipsed by that day were home telling their spouse they felt the same way.

Fortunately, Darcy didn't view the situation the same way I did. And it wasn't just newlywed idealism. She figured the smart people in the admissions department at Dallas Seminary knew what they were doing. She also believed that résumés and pedigrees hold only a minor position when it comes to a person's ultimate potential. But most importantly, she believed that "he who began a good work in [me would] perfect it until the day of Christ Jesus" (Philippians 1:6 NASB).

But her perspective didn't change the dilemma I was facing. The next day, my "I'm in over my head" attitude morphed into a case of insecurity on steroids. That's when they started passing out the syllabuses at the start of the semester. By the time I finished reading the last one on my second day of classes, I figured I was already three weeks behind. Welcome to grad school.

Early in that semester, the school offered an event for spouses designed to give them some connection to campus life, as well as an understanding of academic expectations. Dr. Gene Getz was one of the professors chosen to address the spouses that evening. Darcy pulled him aside afterward and explained the dilemma she was facing as a wife who wanted to encourage her husband. Dr. Getz was working on a book at the time—a book that would end up being a national bestseller called *The Measure of a Man*.[1] He gave Darcy a vision for being a wife who made it her aim to build a significant sense of purpose into her husband. Over the years, we've learned that this commitment is a two-way street.

Standard Obstacles

It's hard to build a sense of significance into someone else when you don't feel significant yourself. When I speak of significance, I'm not talking about the natural confidence or even cockiness some people have about their personal value. Natural confidence is often a by-product of personality type or even birth order, yet not necessarily backed by performance. In that sense, it's just bravado. And cockiness never wins the day either. What I mean by *significance* is a healthy view of who you are and what you have to offer as a person created by God and paid for by his Son on the cross.

This reality should give us an enormous sense of value. As David said in Psalm 139:14, "I praise you because I am fearfully and wonderfully made; your works are wonderful, I know that full well." The apostle Paul doubled down on this issue when he said, "We are God's handiwork, created in Christ Jesus to do good works, which God prepared in advance for us to do" (Ephesians 2:10). But he didn't stop there. Listen to this: "It is God who works in you to will and to act in order to fulfill his good purpose" (Philippians 2:13).

God didn't create us by accident or empower us at random. He made us to make a difference. When we do, we not only fulfill his purposes but push glory toward him in the process. And we compound our capacity for significance even more when we turn "making a difference" into a byline of our marriage relationship.

Darcy knew that if she was going to live out God's grace in our marriage by building a significant purpose into me, she had to start by letting God fill her own need for a significant purpose. She started a deliberate crusade to help me see myself the way God does rather than the way I perceive others do. And remember, I was the one in seminary, not her. The point is you don't need advanced degrees to figure out how to do the obvious.

Four years later, in the closing weeks of my final semester before graduation, Darcy and I reflected on how different things were from when we arrived in the Big D four years earlier. Darcy was sitting across the table from a man who had learned how to do a much better job of playing his assigned position in life. I appreciated and respected the accomplishments of others, but I realized I was much more useful when I looked beyond the accomplishments and focused more on the needs of the person. I also had accepted the capacities God had given me to learn, love, and live.

I still had light-years of distance between who I was and what I could become through God's grace (and I'm far from there yet). But at least we were moving in the right direction.

What Darcy willingly did for me inclined me to return the favor. We've hit potholes and run off into the ditch many times along the way, but God's grace infused into our marriage has made it a lot easier to recover from these setbacks.

When a husband believes in his wife's significance and uses his love for her as an opportunity to fuel her capacity, their life together becomes more attractive for everyone. And vice versa. Too often, myopic husbands limit their vision for their wife to that of a lover, mother, and date-night companion. Too often, narrow-thinking wives limit their vision for their husbands to a provider, protector, and sperm donor. Without grace, neither can see that a significant purpose is right in front of them. All they need to do is dig for it.

Which brings up another reason that some couples find it hard to build a significant purpose into each other: they've allowed so much residue to build between them that they couldn't care less if their spouse has any of their needs met, including their need for a significant purpose. Fortunately for me, it was too early in our marriage to have backed up much of a reservoir of residue!

Multipurposed Significance

The more you sense you're contributing to the big picture of life, the more significant you feel. The more significant you feel, the more at peace you are with yourself, your spouse, and God. The more at peace you are, the more you enjoy your life and your marriage. It's elementary cause and effect. Making a difference in people's lives yields a greater sense of personal value. When you make it your aim to do all this through the power and presence of Christ, your sense of significance becomes second nature. This frees up your heart to be used by God in enormous ways—like being an ongoing ambassador of his grace to your spouse. Your sense of significance is far from personal pride. If anything, you're aligning your sense of value to your position as a redeemed member of God's family.

Based on that paragraph you just read, would you say you feel intrinsically valuable? Let's slip a little closer to home: Would you say the current dynamic between you and your spouse is pointing your significance fuel meter toward full or empty? If your spouse is not raising your sense of significance, I'm going to suggest something that could change that for you.

The best way to turn your spouse into someone who makes you feel more significant is for you to dedicate yourself to making your spouse feel more significant. This seems counterintuitive, but it is possible when you look at your spouse through the Grace Lens. If you treat your spouse the same way God treats you as a spouse, you will show your spouse grace regardless of whether they deserve it . . . or return the favor.

This is easier if we clarify the dimensions in which a significant purpose can be realized. Before I list some, I'd like you to meet Dan and Ann. They're really good-looking. They told me.

I first met them when they were deciding whether to marry each other. What I most remembered about that introduction was how much they complimented each other's looks . . . out loud . . . to anyone who wanted to listen. There's nothing wrong with a couple being taken with each other physically. That's fairly normal. But for Dan and Ann, physical appearance was all they focused on. I hoped that they would expand their attraction to each other beyond the depth of each other's skin.

The next time our paths crossed was a few years after they had gotten married. They continued to compliment each other's looks. I believe they meant well, but it came across as a bit misguided. It's one thing for a couple to compliment each other's looks privately, but it's another thing for them to go overboard publicly. That usually sends a text message to everyone around them that their love might be missing some vital moving parts.

On a brief visit to their home a few years later, I was surprised to see that Dan had a full-length picture of his nude wife hanging on the wall of his study. Had this been a private thing off the beaten path in his home, I guess to each his own. But this was just off the entryway into his house. You couldn't miss it. I acknowledged the obvious: "You sure are proud of your wife."

"I am," he said, "She's gorgeous."

I wondered if he was proud of her *body* rather than *her*.

I cared for Dan and Ann. I didn't want to see their marriage fail. So I talked with Dan about the wisdom of hanging a picture of his naked wife near the entryway of his home. We discussed the ramifications for Ann, for their kids, and for their reputation. We talked about the pressure it put on Ann as a wife admired primarily for her looks. And we talked about how he and Ann could reflect the values within their marriage that pointed people toward God. He listened. And the nude picture of Ann ultimately came down—but not because of our discussion. Because they divorced.

Their marriage lasted about twenty years before they went their separate ways. When they parted, they weren't complimenting each other's looks anymore. Although they had a bit more weathered appearance, they were still a handsome couple, as far as handsome divorced couples go. When you see the things that brought them down, it was obvious they hadn't expanded their focus to the higher purposes they could build in each other's lives—purposes far more significant than getting an A on your Christmas card photo. They missed the chance to infuse their marriage with grace by becoming each other's cheerleaders in significant ways.

With this in mind, and before we look at three ways to help our spouse build a sense of significance, I'd like to list some purposes we should encourage our spouse to have in their lives.

A General Purpose

The best road map to follow through life is the clear direction offered from a good example. When you got married, you may not have been thinking about how your life together could make life better for everyone else.

It's a fresh air blowing through a neighborhood when a couple lives for the best interests of those around them. They stick up for the defenseless, protect the weak, fight for the oppressed, and maintain a tender heart for the poor. They notice people, applaud their victories, and come alongside them when life has knocked them down.

These are all direct extensions of God's heart of grace. And when a married couple embraces these qualities as a lifestyle, they can't help but benefit personally within their relationship.

Micah 6:8 picks up the chorus of this song with these words: "He has shown you, O mortal, what is good. And what does the LORD require of you? To act justly and to love mercy and to walk humbly with your God." This is one of the great wedding gifts we can keep on giving over and over to our spouse. When we live out a noble purpose for the sake of others as an individual, and inspire it in our spouse through our example, we build their sense of significance.

A Specific Purpose

We marry people with gifts, skill sets, and abilities. For some people, these features are defined and even refined by the time they get married. If that was your story, good for you! But many people exchange vows with little idea of the contribution they could make in life if they harnessed their assets and used them wisely.

If you had interviewed me on my wedding day about my gifts and skills, you would never have heard the word "writer" come out of my mouth. Let's see . . . I was ADHD before they knew what to call it, worked hard for Bs and Cs, and struggled with dyslexia. I read a lot (still do), but I read slowly (still do). Fortunately, God let me marry someone who saw more in me than I ever saw in myself. Darcy noticed, encouraged, gently prodded, and never stopped believing in me.

Part of our early work in ministry required me to capture brief vignettes on paper. Darcy said to me one day, "You use all five senses when you write. I like that." My response was, "I do?" I was clueless. She felt there was more where that came from, so she put on the mining equipment and dug it out of me. What's ironic is that I had to get married to learn I had potential in a discipline that no one had ever noticed in me. If anything, people had discouraged me from thinking that words would be part of how I might contribute to the bigger picture of life.

Part of your love story is how you come alongside your spouse to help them find their sweet spot. When you view your spouse through the lens of God's grace, you help them hit their highest stride when it comes to their interests, passions, calling, and profession. Often their sweet spot is hidden or has been lying dormant. When you make it a priority to encourage your mate to their highest and best level of contribution, God smiles.

A Relational Purpose

We aren't supposed to exist like private islands hogging up some Caribbean attitude in our own personal ocean. We're part of a huge continental community of people. We haven't been placed here on the earth to be takers, occupying valuable space and sucking up air simply because we can. God placed us here to live lives focused upward and serving outward.

Jesus said, "To you who are willing to listen, I say, love your enemies! Do good to those who hate you. Bless those who curse you. Pray for those who hurt you. If someone slaps you on one cheek, offer the other cheek also. If someone demands your coat, offer your shirt also. Give to anyone who asks; and when things are taken away from you, don't try to get them back. Do to others as you would like them to do to you" (Luke 6:27–31 NLT). One of the ways we gain a sense of significance is by living lives that make it easier for the people around us to live theirs. When you make it your aim to notice your spouse, to care for them, and to bring out the best in them, you increase their stock value as a person, as well as a mate—even when they aren't behaving well.

We can enjoy much more significance when we refuse to carry a grudge, pass on gossip, keep score, whine, complain, nag, or criticize. These things are like bad whiskey to relationships. Grace-filled couples refuse to pass on a legacy of bitterness, mistrust, or bullying. We shouldn't want to do this to each other as a couple, and we cannot let it be part of our repertoire as a couple when dealing with others. We will experience a significant relational purpose when we focus on caring, sharing, encouraging, and forgiving.

Our marriage is a golden opportunity to glisten like diamonds. And when we help build a high priority in our spouse to live in a way that makes a positive impact on the people who surround them, we build their sense of a significant purpose to crown-jewels level.

A Spiritual Purpose

Right out of the starting blocks, God placed an expectation on marriage: "God said, 'Let us make man in our image, after our likeness' . . . male and female he created them" (Genesis 1:26–27 ESV).

God meant us to be reflections of him as *couples*. Have you ever seen one of those movies where a person is looking in a mirror, but through special effects, the image looking back is someone else? That's what marriage is supposed to be like. This wasn't just an expectation for us as individuals. God meant for people to be able to see him when they look at us as couples. And they do, when we let God's truth guide us and his grace temper our hearts—especially when life is trying to body-slam us. Grace-filled marriages operate with an athletic faith and enjoy a muscled resolve to keep on loving no matter what.

Our marriage is not merely an image bearer of God but an image bearer of the unity of God within the Trinity. He said, "Let *us* create man . . ." Think about it: there is no selfish member of the Trinity. The love within the Trinity is always focused outward toward the other members. When people see our love focused outward toward our mate, even when we're processing difficult issues with them, people see *God*. How so? Simple: It's not the default mode of our fallen human condition to be outwardly focused—especially when the other person has done us wrong. But that's what God's grace looks like when we've done him wrong. So when we extend that grace toward each other, people can't help but sense something (more specifically, Someone) greater than us is behind the steering wheel of our life. One of the highest representations of the image of God is a husband and wife serving each other.

When people see a husband and wife relating to each other in a context of God's grace, when they see us go to the foot of the cross when we've lost our way, when they see us still caring for each other when life has given us many reasons to walk out, the gospel is validated. We may never know how much God's grace rubs off of us onto others. But it does. When we take our spiritual purpose to heart, our sense of significance grows eternal muscles. It's what happens when we make it our priority to reflect God's majesty through grace-filled marriages.

We've seen four specific purposes that give depth and richness to our inner need for significance: our general influence, our specific roles, our relational touch, and our spiritual impact. Let's close our discussion on building a significant purpose into our spouse by looking at three specific commitments we can make on their behalf.

Our Spouse Feels a Significant Purpose When We Affirm Them

For over a quarter of a century, Darcy and I have been part of the speaker team for FamilyLife. Their Weekend to Remember events have helped more than a million couples over the years. If you've never gone to one, you need to. If you have, go again . . . and again.[2] Over the years, I've enjoyed a front-row seat at hundreds of these events, and every time I leave feeling stronger in my relationship with God and closer in my connection to Darcy.

But in life, we often have to sip the bitter wine with the good. Events like these involve couples at all stages of marital health. Most who attend are committed couples just needing a tune-up. But there are also couples whose marriages are heading for triage. I'm pleased when marriages are resuscitated through the work God does in them. But I'm equally saddened by those that don't make it.

Because of this, I've talked with more couples determined to divorce than I care to count. I have yet to hear them speak in affirming ways toward each other. Couples whose love is on its last legs don't use the Grace Lens. They don't build each other up. They don't see what the other person gets right. But because I've had such a close seat to so many of these couples, I've been able to see something else. As I work my way through their history, trying to salvage some hope for them, invariably I find that building each other up with words and deeds was seldom a high priority. For many, it was nonexistent.

It's not surprising, then, that each spouse feels so valueless in the relationship. Their sense of significance was smothered early on. They toot their own horn so much because their spouse never played that song for them. But when they voice their broken-heart song about their spouse, you seldom hear anything you'd like to harmonize with:

- "I'm nothing more than a paycheck to her."
- "I'd just as soon be invisible for all he's ever noticed me."
- "She treats me like I fell off the stupid truck, it hit its brakes, and it backed over me."
- "All he sees me as is his little bed toy."

King Solomon wisely said, "A gentle answer deflects anger, but harsh words make tempers flare" (Proverbs 15:1 NLT). Cutting, burning, piercing words of criticism only lead down one path—marital insignificance. Eventually, your marriage doesn't matter anymore. The negative consequences of divorce are trumped by your need to find affirmation somewhere else.

But there's power in encouragement. A person's sense of significance is filled by well-timed, well-placed words that affirm them and build them up. Grace-filled couples make it their mission to notice their spouse's contribution to the relationship. They voice approval and appreciation. But this goes beyond just noticing what a spouse does (which is very important). Affirmation also voices appreciation for what a spouse is:

- "You have a keen imagination."
- "I love the way you light up a room."
- "I always feel safer when you're around."
- "You have an amazing way of turning a house into a home."
- "I can't get over how well you shoulder other people's burdens."
- "I'm so grateful I get to wake up next to you every morning."

Regular reminders of how our spouse adds value to life not only deepens their sense of significance but draws their heart closer to ours. When a spouse goes for weeks, months, even years without hearing from us that we appreciate or care about them, it shouldn't surprise us that their love turns bitter.

However, we need to avoid empty praise. Words of praise that aren't backed up by reality are little more than relational junk food. It's just a matter of time before empty praise moves from nice-sounding compliments to meaningless hot air in the ears of the person on the receiving end.

When we look at our spouse through the lens of God's grace, we can find plenty to affirm in them without having to invent things. When we infuse our perspective with grace, it's amazing what we see as well as what we tend not to see, such as things that annoy or distract us. And when we build that affirmation in our spouse, we increase their stock value in the other dimensions of their life.

I mentioned earlier that I took on marriage and graduate school at the same time. I felt much more prepared for coming home to Darcy each evening than I ever felt going to school each morning. My aptitude for Darcy worked from a higher level than did my aptitude for Greek, Hebrew, and systematic theology. There were times in those first few years where I was really low. I had major papers due on subjects that baffled me and finals looming on information I couldn't seem to remember. During these times, we tried to maintain as normal a life as possible. Darcy had to get up to go to work every morning, so most evenings she'd go to bed while I stayed up into the single-digit hours studying.

One night after Darcy was asleep, I opened one of my textbooks and found a note from her. It contained words I desperately needed to hear—words about how she appreciated my intellect, my character, and my tenacity. It was like sweet tea to a parched throat. She noticed the pressure I was under and made a tangible effort to affirm my significance. I folded that note and put it in my wallet.

On another occasion, I had huge finals facing me. I had pulled several all-nighters getting ready for them. I was heading into my last day of tests for the semester and was completely spent. Darcy had caught a ride to work while I was getting dressed. When I came out to get my keys from my desk, I found a note from my wife expressing confidence in me and appreciation for all my efforts. Once again, I folded that note and put it in my wallet.

I still have those notes. I carried them in my wallet for years. Many times I opened them and reread her words. They continued to work over and over again. I retired that wallet to a drawer in my dresser, but those notes are still in it. Over the years the ink has faded, the edges are worn, and most of the folds on the notes are torn. But I keep them still. They represent more than affirmation. They're visible proof of the power behind a believing spouse and the long-term influence of a significant purpose.

Our Spouse Feels a Significant Purpose When We Give Them Our Attention

For several years, I taught a Bible study for a group of young couples. These couples had one thing in common: each husband played professional baseball. One evening we were discussing a passage in the Bible when one of the wives volunteered some information out of the blue: "My husband is having an affair."

Uh-oh, I thought.

All eyes immediately went to hers. She just sat there for a moment, letting her words seep into all of us. Our eyes moved from her to her husband, who was sitting next to her.

"I know his lover. I see her all the time. I *hate* her!" She spit out the words. "She flaunts their relationship—just shoves the fact that she owns his heart right in my face every time I see her." Every woman in the study was now glowering at him. The men sat stunned.

I'd watched this guy dispatch some of the biggest bats in Major League Baseball. Not this time. His wife had his number. If this had been a game, his ERA was about to get shattered. "You know what I'm going to do? I'm going to kill her." *Oh, here we go.* "I'm going to run over her with my Suburban. I'm going to spread her out all over the driveway, that cute little putter and that driver! I'm going to take all those irons and make sure they can't be identified when I'm done with them. And then I'm going to take that golf bag, that buxom piece of trash, douse it in gasoline, and burn it until it's nothing but ashes."

Oxygen started reentering lungs around the room. Bottoms shifted in seats, and just about everybody who had been sitting with their legs crossed reversed the stack. For the remainder of the Bible study we talked about how to make our spouse feel loved and valuable. This pitcher's wife had defaulted to the same method kids often default to when they think their parents aren't giving them enough attention—namely, negative attention is better than none.

After the study was over, this MLB pitcher pulled me aside and said, "Do you think she was serious? I mean, does she really think I need to stop playing golf on my day off and start spending it with her?" I was amazed his wife hadn't run *him* over with her Suburban. He just wasn't getting it!

A lot of spouses don't get it. They don't understand the connection between building their spouse's sense of purpose and focusing attention on their mate. Yes, we all have to work. And there's a place for hobbies. But a grace-filled marriage factors our spouse into the things that make up our life.

Grace-filled couples give each other access to their schedules and the first right of refusal to major shifts in plans. But it's much more than that. A spouse feels valuable when we notice what they notice, when we care about what they care about, when we know what they're up against and maneuver our time, resources, and focus to be there for them when they need us.

Our Spouse Feels a Significant Purpose When We Give Them Admonition

Admonition is something you do both *to* and *for* your spouse that builds a significant purpose into them. In other words, you admonish your spouse by speaking up when their actions or attitudes need a course correction. And you build their sense of value by respecting their areas of strength so much that you're open to their critique. This commitment says, "I value who you are and what you have to offer to me that will make me a better person." Most couples get married with their personal preferences kept in vaults that cannot be trifled with. But a grace-filled openness to your spouse's admonition makes both of you much better people.

Could our spouse take advantage of this posture in us? Of course, especially if they're letting their fears and inadequacies do the evaluating—and also if they deliver admonition with a my-way-or-the-highway finality. But that kind of admonishment doesn't fly under the banner of God's grace. God gives us all kinds of advice and critique in the Bible. Sometimes his concerns are delivered with urgency. But he never demands, threatens, or insists that if we don't comply, he'll withhold his love.

The balancing feature is grace. When grace leads the way in admonition, a couple can help each other become much more effective people.

Darcy and I didn't live together before we were married. When I was at her house, her dad made it clear that I was never to be in her bedroom for any reason. Had I visited her room, I would have learned a lot about the kind of environment she prefers—bed made, clothes hung up, shoes organized, and everything in its proper place. Had she ever visited my room, she would have noticed it was decorated in the "gravity look"—wherever things landed was fine with me. I wasn't a slob. In fact, I prefer order. But because I tended to run late and my mind was usually elsewhere, my room typically had more of a "nest" feel to it. I'd clean it up occasionally, but disorder didn't bother me. Disorder bothered Darcy a lot. I could thrive in either environment, but she could only thrive in one.

Then we got married. At night I would get undressed by gravity. The next morning, I'd climb out of bed and proceed with my day. In the evening, I'd return home and my clothes would be hung up, shoes put on a shelf in the closet, and the bed made. Frankly, I didn't really notice it. It didn't matter to me one way or the other.

One evening as I was letting gravity help me undress, Darcy walked out of the closet with a determined look on her face and a clothes hanger in her hand. I thought, *That's going to leave a mark!* But she didn't have anything menacing on her mind. She said, "Tim,

I need us to make a permanent change in our arrangement here. I'm glad to be your wife, but I can't be your maid. I'd really like you to hang up your clothes at the end of the day and put your shoes in the closet where they belong. I'd like you to help me keep our room clean and straightened up." Then she said, "And how about we team up to make the bed every morning? If one is up and gone, then the last one out is responsible. If we're both here, we can each take a side. But we're going to keep our room and our home nice. I need this to feel calm, and I think you'll do better in an orderly home too."

She could have rented a hazmat suit to demonstrate how nasty the job was of cleaning up after me. She could have cranked up the leaf blower in the bedroom to show how frustrating it was to get all my clothes from under the bed blown into the closet. She could have mocked, insulted, brow-beaten, or nagged me about my selfishness. But she didn't. Sure, she needed an orderly home, but she also knew I would thrive in one too. Grace tends to default to the highest common denominator rather than the lowest.

I recalibrated my procedures right there. A lot of it had to do with how cute she looked coming at me with that clothes hanger. But also, she was right. We both had strengths to bring to the relationship, just as you and your spouse do. If we were open to the other person's evaluation—seeing it as a gift within a bigger package—we would all feel far more significant.

But that was a tame example involving housekeeping etiquette. It gets a lot tougher when our spouse is admonishing us in an area of obsession, delusion, or sin. Yet grace must speak up in these areas. Silence isn't golden when you're watching the person you love heading off a cliff. Grace says, "I love you too much to watch you self-destruct. I love you too much to protect myself by staying silent. I'm going to speak up when I think you or we are off course. It's not because I need or want my way. It's because grace compels me."

I wish I had learned to respond to Darcy's admonitions over the years as well as I did to the one about keeping our room tidy. The truth is, lots of sparks fly in this area of a married couple's relationship. And many times they fly not because of what the critique is about but how it's delivered. Grace is kind and gentle. It isn't delivered with snarls and threats. Grace doesn't look at things with a scorecard in hand. Grace treats your spouse the way God treats his. God loved the church so much, he wrote almost the entire New Testament as an admonition. That's because God wants a spouse who lives out a significant purpose—a kingdom purpose. If he thinks it's a good idea for his spouse, I think it goes without saying, it's a brilliant idea for all of us married people. So how are you doing when it comes to accommodating your spouse's preferences? And when it's time to speak tough things to your spouse, do the words coming out of your mouth sound like grace or more like the words of a grouch?

Your commitment to *affirm* your spouse, to give them focused *attention*, and to *admonish* them in a spirit of grace will go a long way toward building a sense of significant purpose into their heart. These gracious efforts cost us so little but produce more than we can quantify in our spouse over a lifetime.

———

CHAPTER 6

Grace Gives You a Strong Hope

—

Everybody gets married with a certain capacity to weather life's storms. Some show up at the altar with a measurable track record of tenacity. Whether due to their family of origin, their choices, or their knack for drawing the short straw in situations, they've been forced to build their inner strength.

The upside is that we know these people already have a lot of true grit. Life has hit them hard over and over again, and they're still standing . . . with a calm, contented smile.

But this isn't the way it is for most people. Most tend to take the safe and well-traveled trails on life's journey prior to exchanging wedding vows. So even though your capacity for inner strength may have had some exercise, it's hard to know going into marriage how you and your spouse are going to handle the collisions with life.

When we realize that we lack strength in dealing with difficulties or find out our spouse's voids when it comes to inner strength, we need a commitment to tap into God's grace.

Grace may be the only way out of it all.

Officer Down

There's a precious couple that comes to my mind. The biggest test of their marriage came before it even started. While she was scratching through her wedding checklist, he was recording his early successes as part of an elite police force. If you had known them at this time, you would have agreed they were both high-capacity people. But neither knew the challenge their new marriage would endure.

There's nothing routine about a major police raid on a hideout of bad guys. The checklist my friend and his fellow officers were using would have made his bride-to-be's wedding checklist look more like a "nice try." Outsiders can only imagine the training, anticipation, and what-if exercises required to send police officers into a zone filled with deadly unknowns. But when these policemen moved into position, they were confident they had done their homework well.

Sometimes, when homework is a group project, the finished product is only as reliable as the weakest link. There was a piece of vital information that got confused along the way. When the police invaded the complex, decisions had to be made in split seconds. In the midst of the shouting and shifting between the good guys and the bad, an undercover officer who was already inside was unwittingly killed. This young groom-to-be found himself facing one of the most haunting realities a police officer could ever suffer—he had accidentally shot and killed a fellow officer.

In the immediate aftermath of this tragedy, the maturity and character of this young man carried him through the investigations. Yet he was devastated by what had happened. Their wedding proceeded on schedule but with a cloud of sadness hanging over it for him. They tried to get things off to a good start, but neither bride nor groom realized the curtain that the "officer down" event had pulled between them and the joy that should have accompanied their new life together.

Interestingly, his true reaction to the tragedy got shoved deep within him and, like a terrorist sleeper cell, lay dormant for years. That can be the nature of post-traumatic stress. It wasn't until they were years into their marriage that he realized his limited capacity for inner strength. When his pain and shame came out of hibernation, it showed itself as anger, frustration, and the withholding of affection toward his wife. If you know much about these kinds of events, most of the time, there's a divorce-court scene before it's over.

But this man had married a woman who believed in a divine grace that was bigger than human disgrace. She knew that neither she nor her husband could ever exhaust God's love. She chose to fill her marriage with that grace and love throughout the emotional explosions . . . the physical rejection . . . the canyons of depression. And she chose to take this grace-filled path for years. That's how long it took for his shame and regrets to work their way out enough that they could finally be dealt with.

A wife chose not to give up on her husband by tapping into the same grace God extended when he chose not to give up on us. God's grace sustained her through the lonely years, and God's grace helped fill the void in her husband's inner need for a sense of strength.

A Strong Hope

God is in the hope business. And that's a good thing. Last time I checked, there's a lot of despair making its way around. Like a stubborn flu strain, discouragement has a way of moving back and forth between a husband and wife until there's no one left to run to the pharmacy. Fortunately, God still makes home deliveries. He wants to give us the strength to face the everyday challenges that come our way, as well as a hope to carry us through circumstances that are bigger than any person is equipped to face.

God knows us better than we could ever know ourselves. After all, he made us. He built into us a need to know we're *secure, significant*, and *strong*. But he also knew that in any of these categories, we would all meet our match. Human capacity only goes so far. That's why he meant for these needs to be met in team with him and in concert with the people closest to us.

We've learned about the confidence available through a *secure love*, and the value we feel when we know we have a *significant purpose*. We finish this trio of inner needs with a look at the calm God wants to wash over us through a *strong hope*—a hope that only he can guarantee. Grace-filled marriages recognize this need for a strong hope and help spouses with holes in this area to see beyond their fears.

The Fear Factor

We all have a tendency to focus on the waves breaking around us as we try to walk across the water to Jesus. The Goliaths of life don't have to cross our paths, just their shadows . . . or the rumors that they're nearby looking for a fight. In situations like these, it's second nature for many with a low strength quotient to have a difficult time mustering much courage.

It can be even more frightening as you try to face your fears as a couple. Your confusion as parents, your shortcomings as providers, and ineptness as partners can leave you nursing an epidemic-size case of inadequacy. That's why as grace-filled couples, we need to make it our aim to always keep the work of Christ on the cross in our vision.

When we revisit God's work for us at Calvary, he helps us gain the strength and hope we need to process life's setbacks. Listen to Paul as he layers brick upon brick of God's truth with the mortar of hope that we have in Christ:

> Therefore, having been justified by faith, we have peace with God through our Lord Jesus Christ, through whom also we have obtained our introduction by faith into this grace in which we stand; and we exult in hope of the glory of God. And not only this, but we also exult in our tribulations, knowing that tribulation brings about perseverance; and perseverance, proven character; and proven character, hope; and hope does not disappoint, because the love of God has been poured out within our hearts through the Holy Spirit who was given to us. (Romans 5:1–5 NASB)

Christ came to take the fear out of our fear factors. He gave us access to his heart of forgiveness and his work of reconciliation through his grace so that we could (among other things) be set free from the tyranny of our fears. We know how the story of history finishes. He tells us in his Word. What he started at the cross reaches its ultimate expression as we gather in his presence in heaven. He wants to give us hope when it comes to facing everything in between.

And "hope does not disappoint." Jesus has given us a hope through his grace that won't let us down. The grace that saves us from our sin has the power to sustain us through our setbacks. And with this, he wants to pour out his love within our hearts through the power and presence of the Holy Spirit within us. The way his hope is revealed in people who have let God's grace empower them and his hope sustain them is a peace that "exceeds anything we can understand" (Philippians 4:7 NLT).

Do you operate in a default mode of hope? How about you as a couple? If not, you might need a deeper understanding of God's grace.

Fear-Filled Marriages

When people spend a lot of time focusing on the things they fear, they have a hard time looking optimistically at the present, let alone the future. And they shouldn't be surprised that they lack confidence in God's ability to sustain them and protect them. I've known many couples who deprive themselves of joy by worrying about things that aren't as serious as they make them out to be, or things they can't do anything about.

It's sad to see the long-term damage that fear can do to a couple. One evening Darcy and I were sitting across a table in a restaurant from two people we had recently gotten to know. They had kids about the same ages as ours, so we were really looking forward to the evening.

It's a good thing we had the option to order off the menu, because if this couple had been in charge of our dinner, we would have had *worry* for hors d'oeuvres, a salad of *angst*, a main course of *the sky is falling*, and finished off with some chocolate-covered *it's the end of the world as we know it*. These were two extremely fearful people. But it didn't add up. They weren't from distressed families with disturbed childhoods. They weren't spiritual newcomers either. Their faith stories went all the way back to their childhoods. But to hear how intimidated they were by the world around them, the greater biblical message didn't seem to have influenced their perspectives.

They had concerns about things I hadn't given a second thought. They went from Hollywood to music to the Internet to cohabitating neighbors. Regardless of what Darcy and I said to put their concerns in balance or perspective, they held fast to their negative worldview. Just when I thought we had exhausted their list of fears, the husband changed the subject. He was adamant about not letting any of his kids in the public schools in their district. He described his visit to one of the campuses and couldn't elaborate enough on all of the reasons he felt that no parent in their right mind would send their kids there.

During one of his pauses, I mentioned that all our kids were in those public schools and added that they were thriving spiritually— not surviving but thriving. I tried to show him how to put on a Grace Lens so he could see that no matter how we educate our children, the basis of our choice should never be fear. Darcy and I tried to help him see past his fears by pointing him to scriptures like "The one who is in you is greater than the one who is in the world" (1 John 4:4). But our friend's mind, and fears, were made up. Nothing we said nudged him away from his certainty that there was much to be concerned about in the world. The fact that we have a sovereign God who is greater than any of our concerns did not resonate with him.

This man made the mistake so many make. He let his fears own the high ground in his perspective. His wife followed his lead, thinking he must have good reason to be so fearful. Rather than assuring her of God's care and his protection, he fed her anxieties and sucked the joy out of their marriage.

When we don't have a strong sense of hope, we, by default, become high controllers. High control is leveraging the strength of your personality or your position against weaknesses of others in order to get them to meet your selfish agenda.[1]

When we invite fear, doubt, or worry to occupy seats in the boardroom of our heart, all kinds of things can wreck the joy of our marriage. We live in a state of reaction, which robs a wife of her security and a husband of his confidence. God didn't mean for it to be that way.

Scripture says, "God has not given us a spirit of fear and timidity, but of power, love, and self-discipline" (2 Timothy 1:7 NLT). God wants us to operate in an attitude of faith that shows itself in an ongoing ease at *trusting* him. You might want to read that sentence again. God knows what we're up against. He understands police raids gone wrong, a culture that denounces faith, and schools that present challenges.

He built into us a need to know we're strong and took the steps necessary to assure us that we have every reason to place our hope in him. The way we measure our level of inner strength is by how quickly we default to calm and confidence in the Lord's power to lead, sustain, and protect us in any given situation. This is why we must allow God's grace to temper our hearts. The primary feature of a heart of grace is that it lives to *trust* God. It operates from a position of humility that frees it up to place its confidence in the mighty hand of the Lord.

Litmus Tests

I can tell when a couple's sense of inner strength is high or low simply by how at ease they make me feel when I'm around them. Are their hearts open or guarded? Do they see a change of plans as a crisis or simply as a change of plans? Do they view an unknown primarily as a risk or an opportunity? When they talk about their struggles in general, do they voice words of confidence or intimidation? Do they convey a sense of vigor or weakness about the challenges in their life? Do they sound as if they're taking their cues from the Word of God or from the latest cable news update? Marital love can blossom and grow only when it envisions a hopeful future.

I see two types of couples who fall into the negative side of these contrasts. Either both spouses have a low degree of strength and hope, or one does and the other accommodates that spouse's ability to stay that way. However, if love is the commitment of your will to your spouse's needs and best interests regardless of the cost, how is enabling your spouse to stay intimidated, weak, or fearful in their best interests? How is the personal cost to you of pulling your spouse out of a state of inadequacy too high of a price to pay? As a grace-filled spouse, you cannot be willing to resign your mate to a mediocre relationship with God and guarantee that your spouse will make little to no contribution to life in general. That's not very loving . . . or gracious.

Grace-filled couples don't deny the reality of the clear and present dangers that surround them. They realize that God gave them brains that he expects them to use when negotiating the rocks and shoals of life. And just because we're processing life through a filter of confidence in God doesn't mean we don't get pangs of fear about real dangers or sadness over setbacks. It just means these don't dictate our "What next?" scenarios.

A low strength quotient in a marriage steals the joy of the relationship. An intimidated mind-set keeps couples from enjoying their work, their money, their time, their friends, their kids, and each other. And worst of all, fear keeps couples from enjoying their relationship with God. It denies them the box seat to his mighty work. It also keeps them from being used by him in substantive ways to make an eternal difference.

I like the way Jesus' half brother Jude drove home this point: "To him who is able to keep you from stumbling and to present you before his glorious presence without fault and with great joy—to the only God our Savior be glory, majesty, power and authority, through Jesus Christ our Lord, before all ages, now and forevermore!" (Jude 24–25).

This passage doesn't mean we won't have setbacks or stumble on our journey through life. We all will. We all do. And some of our setbacks are unimaginable. Jude is saying that no matter what, God won't let us fall out of the reach of his mighty arm or beyond the limits of his attending mercy. His glory, majesty, power, and authority aren't gifts he saves for our future but extensions of his grace that he makes available to us around the clock.

Grace-filled couples need to know this. They need to practice this reality by exercising confidence in God when everything around them and in them is telling them to panic. When they embrace this strong hope, it will free them to embrace their love for God and for their spouse. When one member of the wedding duo has a tougher time doing this, it presents a wonderful opportunity for the person with a greater reserve of inner strength to be an agent of grace to their spouse. Darcy and I know this from personal experience.

Whereas I was raised by a father who demonstrated great faith in the midst of financial and health challenges, Darcy did not have an example of spiritual faith growing up. As a result, in some of the challenges we've faced as a married couple, Darcy has turned to me to gently remind her of God's faithfulness and goodness.

Fortunately, there are specific grace-filled exercises we can add to our marriage that empower us to use our words and actions to help build a strong hope into our mate. Just as in the past two chapters, we'll use three words that start with the letter *A* to give us direction.

Our Spouse Feels a Strong Hope When We Encourage Their God-Given Abilities

I wish you could meet my friend Kit. Our paths first crossed when she was just out of college. She was born into a gentrified family in Arizona. This birthright afforded her the freedom to pursue the path of least resistance in life. But Kit felt she had a clear calling. It tugged at her heart through her upper-crust childhood.

She saw the disenfranchised and noticed how many of them had little or no options for changing their circumstances. Plus, she had read the Bible enough to know that God wasn't silent on this issue. With more than two thousand verses about the kind and just treatment of the poor, God had made his expectations clear.

Right around this time, Kit fell in love with a great man. Wayne was a man's man. He was the kind of guy you'd choose first for your football team and to have your back in a bar fight. He knew how to lead, love, and provide for his family. But the more days he woke up next to Kit, the more he saw in her a higher and better contribution she could be making. However, for her to make that contribution, he would have to take a position beside her, often covered by her shadow.

The dream they realized was a joint effort. But it needed a voice to lead the way, so Kit became that voice. She became the primary brand of a ministry to the underserved parts of Phoenix called Neighborhood Ministries.[2] For over a third of a century, it's been Jesus' hands and heart to thousands of families within the inner city of Phoenix. All along, you could hear Wayne's voice in the background cheering Kit on, his hands applauding her victories, his tears sharing her defeats. He's always played a role in this work, but his greater role was to make sure Kit was free to do all God had called her to do.

Neighborhood Ministries dispenses hope. Over the years, thousands of people have been given a chance at something that would have otherwise been unavailable to them. You can't count how many young people have been given a future that didn't have to include jail time. And you can't count how many young people got a second chance when it did. Everything in this ministry has come with gospel gift-wrapping. Kit's efforts can't be quantified.

But as someone who got to see it from the beginning, I realize the critical role Wayne played. Had he discouraged Kit's pursuits, marginalized her attempts, or denied her access, so many would have lost so much. But God's grace flows from this man's heart. His commitment to encouraging a strong hope in his wife has enabled thousands of poor and desperate people to enjoy a strong hope too.

The apostle Paul said, "We are God's handiwork, created in Christ Jesus to do good works, which God prepared in advance for us to do" (Ephesians 2:10). God has placed abilities in all of us. He meant for us to ID these early on and then maximize them for his glory and the benefit of others. When we do this, we feed our need to feel a strong hope. We get to enjoy the fact that God has given us a position to play in the game of life, and he'll empower us to play it well.

When we connect the dots between having a strong hope and harnessing our spouse's God-given abilities, the strength of our marriage increases exponentially. Together we become greater than the sum of our parts. This is why we've got to be honest about the toxic power we wield in our spouse's life when we mock their dreams or disparage their attempts to try something new.

There's an old adage that says, "You're either doubled or halved on your wedding day." Grace-filled couples quadruple each other's potential. In the process, the strength of their marriages, and the hope they offer to others, allows them to leave their footprints all over the future—even long after they're gone.

Our Spouse Feels a Strong Hope When We Encourage Them toward Great Accomplishments

It's sad when you see people too afraid to dream, too afraid to try something new, or too afraid to fail. Sometimes the only thing holding a person back from developing a strong hope is the lack of encouragement. Maybe they came from a long line of people who were great at starting things but lousy at finishing them. Or maybe they've had some setbacks that made them believe their big dreams could never come true. Pulling people out of these free falls often requires a lot of encouragement.

Like the guy I heard about whose dad died his sophomore year of college, and he had to drop out in order to manage the family business. Although he did his best, his heart was never truly in this work. He struggled for almost two decades with discouragement. Each year that passed subtracted from the internal strength and hope he had going for him back before he got that tragic call that took him off course toward his dream of being a teacher.

Fortunately, he married wisely. His wife refused to stop believing in him long after he already had. She kept helping him revisit his dream and encouraged him to finish college. It's tough enough to get a teacher's credential, but it's even tougher to get a job with one when you're just starting out in your forties. But he did. By the end of his third year of teaching, he received the coveted Teacher of the Year award from his students. The reason his students chose him was because of the way he encouraged them to dream big dreams and then go make them happen. If they had known him ten years earlier, they would not have heard any such message from him. Fortunately, he compounded his potential on his wedding day; it just took about twenty years for the math to hit home in his heart.

We need to become mentors to our spouse. They need to know we believe they can do the things God calls them to do, and they need to know we're there to help them see these callings through to completion.

Some coaches gain winning records by using ridicule, shame, and intimidating bravado. Their victories generally come at a high personal price to their players. And usually, before it's over, their accolades are overshadowed by their bad reputation. This is *not* how God coaches his team. He motivates by love. A married couple is a team. Their accomplishments in life depend far more on how they function as a couple than how they perform individually.

Because of this, grace compels us to bring passion, mercy, and encouragement to our role as our spouse's mentor. Mentors sometimes have to ask hard questions or dismiss poor excuses. But everything is done with God's heart leading the way. When we let the grace that overcame our own weaknesses redefine us, we become a grace-filled person committed to seeing our spouse turn their life into a series of positive accomplishments.

Darcy and I know couples who have put drug addiction, financial ruin, alcoholism, adultery, incarceration, and scandal in their rearview mirror for good—all because one spouse didn't give up on the other. They allowed God's grace to build a strong hope where there was only despair. And because of it, we're *all* beneficiaries.

Our Spouse Feels a Strong Hope When We Help Them Live a Life of Adventure

Writers love to put people in categories. So, my turn.

People either want to be spectators or players. Spectators pay to sit in seats that are a safe distance from the action to watch others take on the big challenges of life. Players, on the other hand, get paid to take on those challenges. They may not get paid financially, but they enjoy a reward that cannot be gained by those who merely watch without risk. Spectators are usually quick to criticize. In fact, criticism seems to go hand in hand with choosing the path of least resistance. Players, however, are too busy tackling their next challenge to enjoy the luxury of throwing around cheap condemnation.

With this contrast as our background, let's drive a stake in the ground about something everyone can agree on: one of the best ways to build a strong hope into our spouse, and our marriage, is to live a mighty adventure. I'll take it a step up from there: one of the best ways to build a strong hope is to live a mighty *spiritual* adventure. When our primary desire is to be emissaries of God's grace, any adventure we take on is a spiritual adventure.

Adventures require taking risks, facing unknowns, and processing fear. Last time I checked, risks, unknowns, and fear are things God loves to lead us through. You can't live a life of genuine faith without being willing to follow God into places you'd prefer to avoid—trusting him all the way.

When we insist on a married life of minimal risks, we choose safety over strength. God doesn't want us to live a safe life; he wants us to live a strong one. To do that, we have to be willing to listen to the prompts he gives us when he wants us to turn onto the roads less traveled. It's not uncommon for one member of the marriage team to be more inclined toward this than the other. And obviously, adventure doesn't give anyone license to be reckless. But there is a cause-effect between a sense of strong hope and couples who are willing for God to use them to do mighty things.

One of the things you have to know when you choose to live a life of adventure is that you're going to be defeated. Victories in life are almost always a process of two steps forward, one step backward. Undefeated seasons are anomalies. So it is with a married couple who ends up in the winner's circle. You seldom get into it without scars to show for your effort. But what's the alternative? You can take the safe spectator's route through life where you never have to lose, but you never gain much of anything either. Or you can take on the risks of life knowing that you will be forced to lean into each other and lean into the Lord in ways you never would have otherwise. Leaning into each other is a good thing. It's even better when you're both leaning into God at the same time.

Paul urges us in 1 Corinthians 15:58, "With all this going for us, my dear, dear friends, stand your ground. And don't hold back. Throw yourselves into the work of the Master, confident that nothing you do for him is a waste of time or effort" (MSG).

The confidence we bring to our daily challenges and the hopeful perspective we have toward life are directly connected to our willingness to trust God. When we do, he isolates our strength need and turns it into spiritual steel, whether our challenges are pint-size or wear sandals that could fit Goliath. With this sense of strong hope, grace-filled couples will be used by God to do mighty things.

—

CHAPTER 7

Grace Frees You to Be Different and Vulnerable

———

It's time to get even more practical in our discussion on grace-filled marriage.

Not that we haven't been dealing with the daily how-tos of bringing the best out of each other. Our discussion of the three driving inner needs was foundational to getting to where we are now. In fact, when we're committed to building a secure love, a significant purpose, and a strong hope into our spouse individually, and our marriage collectively, these other features of applied grace (which we're about to learn) come much more easily . . . and naturally.

The three driving inner needs are like bedrock for a marital love that goes the distance. And the primary *source* of our secure love, significant purpose, and strong hope is Jesus. *Nobody* has what it takes to meet the demands of love on their own steam. Everybody hits the wall somewhere along their journey. We all need something— more specifically, *Someone*—bigger than ourselves to meet the challenges love brings our way. When we allow Christ to be the definitive Rock on which we build our marriage—taking our cues from his grace-filled heart along the way—we're ready to weather whatever may come.

What we need now is a delivery system for grace—a *climate* that allows love to reach its highest potential in our marriage. After all, love doesn't thrive well in confinement. Most things don't. A highly restricted heart—especially one selfishly manipulated by someone else—goes into a slow shutdown. Love was meant to bask in the sunlight, walk around naked, dance without inhibitions, and process its shortcomings in the open. The one place where this was supposed to hit its high-water mark was within the covenant of marriage. That's why it's so important to invite God's work of grace to be a defining feature of our commitment to each other.

And just as your marriage has a personality, God's grace has a personality. You know when you're around grace. When you breathe it in from the person closest to you, your spirit tends to smile. Grace makes people feel more confident, more inclined to contribute to the direction you're mutually going, and more determined to work through setbacks you encounter in a spirit of unity. Who wouldn't want grace to be the wind at your back in a marriage?

The Secret Sauce

When we stack hands as a couple on the finished work of Christ on the cross and declare our marriage a legalism-free, performance-free zone, we position ourselves to enjoy a potential and power that knows no limit. I want to show you how to do that as an extension of God's heart of grace. In this chapter you will learn practical, grace-filled ways to bring the best out of your mate—ways that work!

But before we go there, we need to look at the main ingredient in the grace-filled secret sauce. Most of you are going to love it. For some of you, however, it's going to scare the stuffing out of you. Ready?

Freedom.

In John 8:32, Jesus said, "You will know the truth, and the truth will set you free." This truth he was referring to had everything to do with us capturing the heart message of God—the essence of the gospel. And what was that? Well, the first time Jesus preached a sermon in a synagogue, he addressed this very issue. He read Isaiah 61 to the crowd: "God's Spirit is on me; he's chosen me to preach the Message of good news to the poor, sent me to announce pardon to prisoners and recovery of sight to the blind, to set the burdened and battered free, to announce, 'This is God's year to act!'" (Luke 4:18–19 MSG).

After Jesus read this, he gave the scroll back to the attendant, sat down, and said, "You've just heard Scripture make history. It came true just now in this place" (v. 21 MSG).

Jesus came to set us free from our sin, as well as to set us free from the futility of trying to measure up to his standards with our man-made add-ons. Here's how he summarized his desires:

> Are you tired? Worn out? Burned out on religion? Come to me. Get away with me and you'll recover your life. I'll show you how to take a real rest. Walk with me and work with me—watch how I do it. Learn the unforced rhythms of grace. I won't lay anything heavy or ill-fitting on you. Keep company with me and you'll learn to live freely and lightly. (Matthew 11:28–30 MSG)

Jesus went to a lot of trouble to set our hearts free. He didn't die on the cross to free us to be able to do whatever we want. He freed us to be able to do what he created us to do without artificially imposed restraints.

This is a huge point when it comes to marriage. The grace that saved us is the grace that's supposed to show up in marriage with un-fettered love and uncluttered devotion. Jesus wants us to show each other a love that doesn't make wrongs out of nothings, doesn't trivi-alize our spouse's feelings, doesn't stifle their concerns, and doesn't withhold mercy when they've lost their way and are trying to get back.

Earlier, we were introduced to a napkin strategy for a grace-filled marriage. It was a house with four levels. In the past three chapters, we looked at the first level listed on that house diagram—meeting our spouse's three driving inner needs. In this chapter and the next, we will unpack that second level of the house and look at four free-doms we can give our spouse as agents of God's grace . . .

- the freedom to be different,
- the freedom to be vulnerable,
- the freedom to be candid, and
- the freedom to make mistakes.

The Freedom to Be Different

Were you and your spouse as surprised by your differences after you got married as Darcy and I were? For Darcy and me, it was as though we were suddenly riding in the same car with someone we had just met.

As I mentioned earlier, couples tend to notice what they have in common more than what they have in contrast when they're dating. We tend to see what we like about the person we're falling in love with rather than what annoys us. Add to this the reality that we are continually morphing to adjust to what life brings us along our journey, and you can see why it's vital that grace-filled spouses give each other the freedom to be different.

The fact is, as married couples, we have to make great adjustments to our passions, tastes, and list of necessities *after* we're married. Before two people get married, they're trying to win each other's hearts. That's why we do many things with our loved one before marriage that we'd rather never do again afterward (like taking long walks on the beach or sitting in a deer stand). It's also why we don't do many things before marriage that we can't wait to start doing again once we're married (like hitting the button on our Waylon and Willie mix or color-draping the dog).

This is why we need to have a grace-filled heart toward each other. Some of the things we did before marriage to win each other's heart are going to grate on each other, even though there's nothing actually wrong with them. Grace-filled couples give each other the freedom to be different.

From Safe to Sorry

There are some things about a mate that, over time, can become a source of irritation. Sometimes it's a mannerism, like the wife with the huge laugh or the man who can't make a simple statement without contorting his face. These are things that are unique to them. They're part of their genetic code. These are things that grace-filled spouses celebrate in their mate! They're the things that make them *them*.

We should never marginalize our spouse for things that are unique parts of their physical or personality makeup—body styles, physical inclinations, personality quirks, and bizarre (albeit benign) interests.

We come in all shapes and sizes, all kinds of likes and dislikes. We need to grant each other the freedom to be who we are. For instance:

- One spouse can't wait for the next installment of some romance series, while the other sets the TV to record the next episode in a zombie series.
- One spouse prefers to overdress for whatever's on the calendar; the other prefers to underdress.
- One spouse likes to sleep in the buff; the other heads to bed looking as if they just fell off the chairlift.

These are personal preferences that define who that person is. If they bother you, grace says, "Get over it, accept it, celebrate it, and protect it!"

Taking It Personally

Unfortunately, grace leaves the building when either spouse insists on imposing their selfish will on the other. And it's nowhere to be found when one spouse tries to moralize the other's benign preferences in good-versus-bad terms.

Grace-filled couples are careful not to make moral issues out of nonmoral things. They're also careful not to make any issue out of a nonissue. All this said, does grace allow you to voice your preference? Of course. You can occasionally say, "You know, an outfit I really like on you is . . ." Or "This party we're invited to is a bit more upscale than your cargo shorts and flip-flops." But grace leaves it at that. It doesn't coerce, shame, embarrass, or condescend to manipulate our spouse toward things that are nonissues. When a culture of grace is truly present in a marriage, it translates into a desire on each other's part to be sensitive and accommodating.

Over the years, Darcy and I have refereed some silly disputes, all because one spouse could not accept the other's nonmoral preferences, mannerisms, or personality quirks. We've seen it get ugly, painful, and humiliating.

I remember one lady's frustration over a difference that was beyond-belief annoying but utterly benign. She and her husband were *city* people. But his job took him to the Midwest, and he let his coworkers talk him into going turkey hunting with them. Next thing she knew, he was hooked. But that's not what frustrated her. The source of her frustration was turkey calling. Turns out her husband had a hidden talent. He was like the Justin Bieber of turkey callers. Who knew? He practiced almost every evening out in the garage as if he was first chair in the *Field & Stream* Symphony Orchestra. To her, it was beyond annoying; it was embarrassing. Then to see his picture, big as a house, on that Bass Pro Shops billboard as their "Special Guest" next Saturday—it made her want to crawl in a hole.

I gently explained to this wife that she needed to look at this through the Grace Lens. Her husband was not asking her to go turkey hunting with him. He didn't practice his turkey calling at the dinner table. He wasn't asking her to stand by his side as he signed autographs at Bass Pro Shops. He just found something he liked to do that wasn't something she would have chosen for him.

We marry people who either have, or develop, interests that are quirky. Grace celebrates these things! That's because grace is connected to the heart of our spouse in such a way that these things become part of the color of their story. It might be a husband cranking away on his turkey call out in the garage, a wife whose laugh can be heard two rooms away, or a husband whose face squinches up when he talks. A grace-filled marriage makes these part of the love story. It's the narrative of uniqueness that makes each of us smile.

Sock It to Me

Sometimes the problem is a point of contention over a behavior in our spouse that in the bigger picture isn't worth making into a major issue. I like the way Scripture nails this home: "Good sense makes one slow to anger, and it is his glory to overlook an offense" (Proverbs 19:11 ESV).

Two different "socks" stories make this point. First, meet Kay and Mike. I'm going to let Kay tell this story in her own words:

> When our girls were very young, we were running on little sleep, and Mike was working long hours trying to provide for us. This was one of the most stressful times in our marriage. When Mike came home, his feet usually hurt. The thing he couldn't wait to do was get out of his shoes and socks. But I was constantly annoyed by the fact that he would often leave his dirty socks lying around . . . on the floor in the entryway, wedged between the couch cushions, in the bathroom, even once on the kitchen counter. I told him how much I hated it when he left his socks lying around, but he continued to do it. And to be fair, it was never out of maliciousness. He'd just take off his shoes as soon as he got home from work, and the socks ended whereever.
>
> What started out as an annoying habit grew into a source of bottled rage for me. I started to see it as a personal affront to my hard work to keep the house clean. This became the pathway to anger in other ways for me. All of a sudden, it wasn't just the socks. He didn't do dishes often enough, he didn't take out the trash often

enough, he didn't help me with the kids enough or offer to make dinner when he had to see how tired I was.

I shared my frustration in my Bible study group. My Bible study leader asked me if I prayed for Mike every day. Honestly, I was too busy caring for the kids to even shower every day, let alone have a few moments to myself to pray for Mike! Plus, I was angry at him. Part of me didn't want to pray for him.

Still, this gentle admonishment kept niggling at my mind. So, I started praying for Mike. Little by little God began to soften my heart toward him. God started to remind me why I loved him. Incidentally, I should add that my husband is a kind, loving, hardworking, faithful man who is head over heels in love with me. He is smart, innovative, and brave. In every way that really matters, he is and always was a good man. God started to point out these greater qualities to me.

One day, after a particularly long night with the girls, I was starting to clean up the morning messes. Of course, there under the coffee table was a pair of Mike's dirty socks. I started to feel the familiar anger creeping up in me. And then I sensed God say, *If something ever happened to him, you would never get to pick up his socks again.*

I lost it. Of course, Lord. Picking up Mike's dirty socks was a reminder that he was here. He was healthy and present with me. The day I don't pick up a pair of his dirty socks may be because he is gone and can never come back. God's grace reminded me that I don't *have* to pick up his dirty socks; I *get* to.

From that day on I saw those sweaty, stinky socks in a new light. They represent a hardworking, good man. And it's amazing how that one small thing transformed so much about our relationship. We started to love each other with a love less entangled in strings. And I am a much more difficult person to live with than he is! Of course, we encourage each other to grow and improve as human beings, but we accept each other—flaws, dirty socks, and all. That's what grace can do in a marriage.

Kay and Mike learned how to appropriate God's grace in their marriage. And grace got them past the small things so that they could truly enjoy the big things.

There's another couple I ran across who would have had a lot more fun if one of them could have learned how to appropriate the power of grace earlier in their marriage. Socks played a big role in their journey, too, but in a different and truly *bizarre* way. It started on their first night together on their honeymoon. It also happened to be the first night they slept with each other. They'd married in the winter, and when they got in bed that first night, things progressed quickly. In the process, they, like most couples, found themselves down to the outfits they were born in—with this exception: she had kept on a pair of cotton tube socks. It was so long ago, she recalls, but she thinks it was just because the room was chilly.

Regardless, their marriage tacked on months and years to its track record. And as with most emotionally healthy couples, their intimate times together also increased. You'd think this would have been a great part of their lives, and it was—for her. But something followed along with them from that first night that became a source of enormous irritation to the husband in this story. It was those socks.

For some reason, that first time with her husband not only gave her a comfortable connection to him but to those tube socks. She became attached to them in the same way a child becomes attached to a blanket at bedtime, except these socks were only called upon to bring confidence to her when she was making love to her husband. She wore them every time—winter, spring, summer, or fall. She'd take them on vacation with her, had them within her grasp on special getaways, and even tucked them into her purse if she and her husband were going to be in a setting where she figured one thing might lead to another. She didn't give it a second thought. She was always ready to slip them on when her husband was in the mood, and she often wore them when she slipped into bed on those evenings when something more than sleep was on her mind. She loved her husband, she loved their intimate life, she loved the freedom they seemed to enjoy, and she loved the fact that she got to enjoy all of it wearing nothing but those socks.

At first, he was so caught up in this new dimension of their relationship that he couldn't have cared less about the socks. But as their intimate life developed its own rhythm and personality, the socks became an uninvited guest to the party. He'd ask her not to put them on. She'd say, "Oh, come on. I feel comfortable in these. I actually feel less inhibited in these. Don't worry about them. Let's just enjoy the moment."

He couldn't let it go. Those socks became his credit-card-size focus. And over the years, those socks had been pulled on, pulled up, and laundered so much that their elastic had long since surrendered. Regardless of the beautiful wife in his arms, all he could think about were those "stupid socks" on her feet. He'd buy her a pretty nightgown to add to the fun of an intimate evening. She'd go into the bathroom to put it on and stand backlit in the doorway for him to see her. He'd look from her beautiful face to her pretty nightgown to "those socks" and then, suddenly, lose the mood.

Ultimately, he pulled away from her. He made those socks his central focus, justifying his physical rejection of her, which ultimately got the two of them in front of a marriage counselor. Fortunately, their issue only took one session to solve. After all, other than this point of contention over the tube socks, everything else in their lives as a couple, and as parents, was healthy.

The good doctor asked the standard opening question, "So why are we all here?" Like a thoroughbred leaping from the starting gates, this husband tore into the story of the tube socks. He picked up the tale from that first night on their honeymoon, walked the counselor through the early days of the socks' role, all the way through the getaways, vacations, and "nooners" where those socks came out. When the husband was finally through, the counselor sat there . . . speechless. Then he turned to the wife and asked the logical question. "Did you bring those socks with you?" She lifted her purse into her lap, snapped it open, and handed them over. "I figured these would be the focus of our discussion, so I brought them along," she said.

The doctor stared at those worn, saggy socks in his hands. Then he looked at the husband and gently said, "Are you *nuts*? You're in here paying me all this money and taking up your wife's precious time complaining that in the midst of your spectacular sex life, your wife feels more comfortable in this pair of tube socks . . . and that *annoys* you? I know husbands who would *kill* to get their hands on this pair of socks if they thought they would have the same effect on their wife! If we could reproduce the impact these socks have on your wife into a line of tube socks, we could be zillionaires! Listen, son. You're married to an amazing woman. From my perspective, these socks should be as high of a priority as your desire to protect your *children*! Please do two things immediately. First, get over the problem you have with these socks. Second, start thanking God every day for them, and for this wonderful wife who loves to wear them when she's blessing you. You're a very fortunate man. If you could see what you truly have, you'd guard these tube socks with your life . . . to the day you die!"

Thankfully, this husband heeded his counselor's advice. In fact, his wife was surprised where she began to run across her socks during the day, like drooped over the mirror in her car, in her makeup drawer, even in the microwave!

Two couples, two points of irritation, both revolving around socks. It's amazing how small things can be the cause of so much unnecessary frustration in a marriage. But it's also amazing how grace can relieve the pressure. For both of these couples, grace saved the day. Both realized that grace-filled couples give their spouse the freedom to be different. Sometimes that looks like sloppiness. Sometimes that looks just plain weird. But when these differences are seen through the perspective of grace, they put a smile on everyone's face.

The Freedom to Be Vulnerable

Besides giving our spouse the freedom to be different, a grace-filled relationship ensures a spouse that they have the freedom to be vulnerable.

As a kid, I remember watching some Westerns where part of the plot was the careful handling of nitroglycerin. The chemical makeup of this volatile agent made it explosive—even deadly—if it didn't receive ongoing TLC. Our spouse's heart is like that.

And for the record, we must be careful to not let our spouse's calm or brave demeanor mislead us into thinking that they're handling things better than they actually are. Stoicism isn't always a sign of emotional strength. Sometimes it's simply a smoke screen concealing an emotional free fall. Muscles and brawn aren't guarantees that someone is capable of processing the emotional challenges in life either. Like the police officer we saw in the previous chapter, you can be Stallone, Schwarzenegger, and Chuck Norris incarnate, but the heart is still extremely fragile when it takes a big enough hit.

Grace-filled marriages recognize that there are things that knock a spouse off their game, things that need to be treated with tenderness, understanding, and patience—things like monthly cycles, pink slips, moving, rebellious children, and bad health reports. We need to create an atmosphere within our marriage where our spouse doesn't feel they have to wear a mask around us to keep from revealing where they are emotionally. They need to know that the deeper hurt or confusion within their heart can come out without fear of being attacked. You know, the way God treats us.

Darcy often hears women lament how their husband never seems to invite them into the inner recesses of his heart. First of all, most men don't do that, at least not naturally. That's a woman thing. So it's true that men tend to play their feelings a bit closer to the chest. However, she's also noticed over the years an ironic response from some of those same women when their husbands actually do bare their hearts to them. For instance, let's say a husband has finally had enough of some particular criticism from his wife, and he says as gently as he can, "Honey, what you just said really hurt me deep down inside." This should be exactly what these women who've been complaining about closed-off husbands have been longing for. But this wife comes back with something like, "I'm picking up unusually high readings of estrogen, Captain. Set tasers for 'dewussify!'" She got what she said she wanted, only to throw it back in his face.

We can't have it both ways. We can't, on one hand, say we want to communicate in more transparent vulnerability and then, when our spouse bares their heart, turn and blow them out of the water at their point of weakness. It doesn't work that way. That's because it wasn't ever supposed to work that way. Usually, a man only has to have his wife do that to him once, and he'll never bare his heart again. He knows it's too dangerous. Scripture warns, "Let your conversation be always full of grace, seasoned with salt, so that you may know how to answer everyone" (Colossians 4:6).

But this goes both ways. When a wife pulls back the curtains on the deeper struggles within her, a grace-filled husband must equally be there holding up a sweater of grace, a jacket of mercy, or a blanket of understanding for her to wrap around her shivering heart.

Listen to how God responds to his spouse: "Cry for help and you'll find its grace and more grace. The moment he hears, he'll answer" (Isaiah 30:19 MSG). He also says, "My grace is sufficient for you, for my power is made perfect in weakness" (2 Corinthians 12:9).

This is how God treats us when we're afraid or lonely or confused or heartsick or sad. Not only does he give us a clear example, but he also gives us equally clear instruction on this matter when it comes to how we're to treat our spouse.

Above all, love each other deeply, because love covers over a multitude of sins. Offer hospitality to one another without grumbling. . . . Use whatever gift you have received to serve others, as faithful stewards of God's grace in its various forms. If anyone speaks, they should do so as one who speaks the very words of God. (1 Peter 4:8–11)

As I said at the beginning of this chapter, marriage must be a safe place for our hearts. Obviously, this isn't giving a green light to unnecessary high drama. Some people confuse being vulnerable with revisiting past hurts over and over. There's nothing grace-filled about that! When a spouse has to keep slipping back into the muck and mire of past disappointments or regrets in order to feel like the discussion is official, that's not vulnerability. That's cruelty. It's also insulting to the *finished* work of Christ on the cross. We worship a God who went to great pains to make it possible for us to live with a clean slate, enjoy new days, and always have a hopeful tomorrow on our horizon.

Even so, life serves up many moments that need God's grace to calm the soul. I remember a time when Darcy really needed a touch of God's grace coming through me. It's the first and only time she had ever been pink-slipped in her life. She had just gotten fired from her primary responsibilities, and it was all because she had, technically, worked herself out of her job.

The scene was the parking lot at Northern Arizona University, moving-in day for new freshmen. We had just finished all the things required to get our youngest son, Colt, set up in his dorm room. We'd made several trips to Target, got his meal plan up and running, met his roommate, and taken him to dinner. We'd done everything we could to ensure he had all he needed to take on this new chapter of his life at a full sprint. Fortunately, we knew the drill. We were veterans, having done this same thing with our three older kids. But this time was different.

Because Colt was the youngest, we were going home to a very different feel than with any of our other kids. His voice would not be calling downstairs to his mother for help finding his football practice equipment, or coming into the kitchen to download his school day each afternoon, or snuggling next to her on the couch in the evening. Although I was feeling some great emotion myself, mine wasn't anything close to what Darcy was processing. One of my primary jobs had been to provide for my kids' needs. I was still very much employed in that assignment. And as long as Colt was in college, my job as provider was going to continue . . . big time.

But for Darcy, this was very different. She had been focused on her job as mother to these kids collectively for almost thirty years. Now, with one hug and kiss good-bye, she was unemployed. Sure, she was still a mom, but the daily role she played in her last child's life was going to radically change. It's supposed to happen this way. There comes a moment when you realize you're moving from being a daily resource to an ongoing reference point in your child's life. She'd trained Colt to stand on his own two feet, to try to make good choices each day, and to face the future with courage. She'd done her job well. He was looking forward to this new phase of his life. But for her, it was a sobering reality that she'd never again get to play the role she had worked so hard to do so well for so long.

She wept off and on throughout our two-hour drive home. I did my best to comfort her. The quiet house and empty chairs at the dinner table hit her deeper and harder in the days that followed, so she needed opportunities to talk and lean into me as she processed her new reality. She didn't wallow in self-pity or mope around with a sad affect. Life was moving on for both of us, and she had plenty to do. But still, her role in life had been redefined, and she had to work through it all. These are times when couples have to lean heavily on the gracious heart of God—and on a grace-filled spouse with whom they have the freedom to be vulnerable.

A marriage has to be a safe place to process the fragile side of your heart. Things change. Sometimes life doesn't add up for us. Couples need to be a safe harbor for each other when they get turned down in life, when those youthful looks or that younger body is gone, when they're not as strong as they used to be, or people don't find them as interesting or as needed as they once were. When there's a seasoned grace in our love, we can process these times with far more class.

Love is fragile. Emotions are tender. There will be times in your journey as a couple where the shadows that cross over your spouse are darker, thicker, and more ominous than you're used to handling. Then there are the quirks and one-off things about your spouse that make them one of a kind. God's grace wants to own these times. His divine heart beats with freedom. That's why grace-filled couples give each other the freedom to be different and the freedom to be vulnerable. It's simply a commitment to treat each other the way God treats us.

CHAPTER 8

Grace Frees You to Be Candid and Make Mistakes

There are two aspects of marriage that tend to generate the most angst in our hearts: how we communicate our deep feelings to each other, and how we process the foolish choices we make individually—choices that often score a direct hit to the heart of our spouse. The blunt-force trauma of these thoughtless words or actions often cause couples to wonder if perhaps going their separate ways is a better idea. A couple might not choose to actually split up, but they can still struggle with deep disappointment in their marriage.

If I can be vulnerable with you, I have to admit that both Darcy and I have been surprised at the stupid things we've said during some of our weaker moments. Along that same line, we can't believe some of the foolish choices we've made in light of the vows we exchanged with each other. Yet even couples trying to pay attention to their vows can find themselves drawing energy from their selfishness in order to deliver some of their most caustic words and pull off their dumbest stunts against their spouse.

One lady has a playlist on her phone that she calls "Songs about the Idiot I Married." She downloaded as many my-husband's-a-loser country songs as she could find. On those occasions when he outdoes himself being selfish or insensitive, she just hits "shuffle" and grinds her teeth. When asked about the wisdom of having something so handy to fuel her frustrations, she said she'd gotten the idea from the playlist her husband has about her on his phone. They have some work to do.

This couple validates an important reality about the truth we're discussing—namely, there isn't one gender that has first position locked up on saying things poorly or acting foolishly toward their spouse. It's human nature to view our marriage with our own best interests in mind. We shouldn't be surprised, then, that we say and do things out of our ego needs or sense of justice and revenge. And it's easy to see how the choices we make with our selfish desires in the driver's seat could easily back over the joy of our spouse.

Driven by Grace

But if Jesus has crossed your path, most likely you'd prefer something better than those toxic words and frustrations that have sniped at your joy since your wedding. Grace compels us to deal with these two areas of our marriage in a way that focuses on Christ's finished work for us and the best interests of our spouse.

Grace can change the dynamic in a marriage by helping a couple commit to using words and actions that appeal to each other's inner needs for a secure love, a significant purpose, and a strong hope. Even if only one spouse is committed to this, it can still make a radical difference. The transforming power that one can have on the other is similar to the transforming power God has on us when he draws us to himself (sometimes kicking and screaming) by meeting our inner needs. In fact, it's identical.

These encouraging words and empowering actions improve the health of the marriage. Yet we all have weak areas and sins that need to be dealt with. This is why we need the next layer in our house of grace—a layer that helps us create a climate of grace that mirrors the one God maintains with his spouse, the church. The air we breathe within this climate is the air of freedom.

In the last chapter, we saw how heart connection is much easier to maintain when we grant our spouse the freedom to be *different* and the freedom to be *vulnerable*. In this chapter, we've come to the areas in marriage that demand grace the most. This is where grace dons its weathered Stetson, scarred steer-wrestling boots, and well-worn work gloves. Grace has to saddle up to deal with two dynamics in marriage that even the best among us are reluctant to surrender to God's control. Although our spouse may want to buck off our attempts to bring grace to this part of their story, the biggest kicks, twists, jumps, and snorts usually come from us.

Bringing grace to our marriage in the two areas addressed in this chapter requires us to swallow our ego, abandon our need for self-protection, and trust God. But if we want to set our spouse's heart free, we've got to add these two freedoms to the list. They might intimidate us at first, but when we allow God's grace to turn them into a boxed set with the freedom to be different and the freedom to be vulnerable, our love can't lose. These two areas of rodeo grace are . . .

- the freedom to be candid, and
- the freedom to make mistakes.

If you have struggled in your marriage with words that have left you humiliated or angry, God's grace wants to do a hard reset on your love. If one of you has brought embarrassment to your reputation as a couple, God wants to give you a gift you don't deserve but desperately need. Let's learn together how to turn these into a grace-filled way of living in your marriage.

The Freedom to Be Candid

Communication is vital to a marriage relationship. We can't be operating in different universes and think we have a chance at the intimacy God designed our marriage to have. A deeply loving relationship between a husband and wife needs to encourage a free exchange of the feelings churning within their hearts. A grace-filled spouse wants to communicate clearly and deeply with their mate, but not pummel their heart in the process.

That's the problem with self-protection. Without grace, we can become so absorbed in making our point that we don't care what effect the delivery of that point makes on the other person. Some couples' ideas of communication are the equivalent of driving in thumbtacks with a sledgehammer. For the record, a sledgehammer can indeed drive a thumbtack into a wall. But in the process, it usually takes out the wall. So we make our point, but we break our spouse's heart in the process. And that doesn't reflect the heart of God.

Some couples think when it's time to say what's on their mind, they can deliver it *Jerry Springer Show*–style. The success of this kind of show is based on the guests' willingness to communicate in complete *honesty*. These shows invite one guest who knows something truthful (yet horrific) about another guest. Then the audience watches with glee the tragic impact this honest information has on the second (but unsuspecting) person. If the exchange goes the way the producer hopes, the ugly truth of one will bring out the ugly truth from the other. Honest evaluations—straight from the gut—will be thrown back and forth, seasoned with insults, expletives, and maybe a few fists. Both participants will feel morally justified because they spoke every word with utter truthfulness. Because the key was letting each other know exactly what they thought or felt, there's also a certain level of satisfaction that each of them was forthright.

Honesty, delivered without any concern for the person receiving it, is usually cruel. This is why I decided to use the word *candid*. Although it sounds like a synonym of *honesty*, it tends to have in mind the dignity of the person on the receiving end. Remember, love has the needs and best interests of the one receiving the candid interaction at heart. For our discussion here, let's agree that *candid* is honesty drenched in grace.

We need this commitment in our marriage because of the simple fact that all couples fight—at least all the honest ones do. We have disagreements, arguments, and back-and-forth exchanges that are required to arrive at understanding. But if our goal is to tell our spouse exactly what we think or feel without any regard for the impact this information will have on them, we end up denying them their dignity for the sake of our own ego satisfaction.

In Ephesians 4:25–32, Paul unpacks the rules for fighting fair. Among other things he says, "Do not let any unwholesome talk come out of your mouths, but only what is helpful for building others up according to their needs, that it may benefit those who listen" (v. 29).

Unwholesome refers to insulting, profane, and denigrating words that may make you feel vindicated but end up feeling like the equivalent of a drive-by shooting to your spouse. Paul tells us to say whatever we need to say in a way that is "helpful"—bringing clarity and mutual understanding. He adds that our candid words should build others up "according to their needs." Oh, that sounds familiar—security, significance, and strength. And at the expense of sounding like a download that's experiencing a digital skip, it makes sense to revisit our definition of *love*: love is the commitment of my will to your needs and best interests, regardless of the cost. The cost might involve not getting to satisfy your selfish desire to tell your spouse what a jerk they are. But God wants our words to build up, not tear down; to heal, not harm; to cleanse, not curse. Paul closes with the exhortation, "that it may benefit those who listen." Grace-filled couples use their candid verbal exchanges to bring out the best in each other. We must do this without marginalizing our spouse or making them feel like they don't matter to us.

Paul adds a point right after this verse that puts our conversations in a bigger spiritual context. He says, "Do not grieve the Holy Spirit of God, with whom you were sealed for the day of redemption" (v. 30).

Paul is pleading his case on the basis of a much larger issue than our relationship as couples—namely, how our verbal exchanges reflect on our greater relationship with God. We're supposed to mirror his image as a couple. The members of the Trinity do not speak disrespectfully to each other. We're supposed to imitate them. On top of that, God put his mark of ownership and protection on us as a result of his work on Calvary. He redeemed us at the cross in order to ultimately redeem us on our spiritual wedding day (in heaven). How we treat each other as a married couple needs to be in line with how he's dealt with us individually.

In the next verse, Paul says, "Get rid of all bitterness, rage and anger, brawling and slander, along with every form of malice" (v. 31).

There's no excuse for our screaming at each other with caustic words. Yelling at someone is a toxic form of high control. Incidentally, it's very effective. Add a contorted face and some cheap-shot names, and pound home your point with profanity, and the person on the receiving end has very few options. Mostly, they cave in.

Only three scenarios are designed for yelling. One is when you're trying to get the attention of someone who is outside the reach of conversational volume. A second reason for yelling is to warn someone of imminent danger. The third is when you're cheering someone on. Other than these three scenarios, there's no reason we should ever scream or yell at someone. When we do, there's a dehumanizing effect on the receiving end. Some spouses defend themselves by screaming back; others by simply curling up inside themselves. Paul says that people who have been transformed by the grace of God need to rise above this kind of rancor.

A Candid Jesus

People in close relationships will always have difficult things that need to be said. Sometimes we have to initiate the conversation; sometimes we're the recipients of it. Between the challenges from kids, schedules, friends, sex, and money, there's no way a couple can get through it all without having to process some tough information. But with a commitment to creating a grace-filled climate where candor can be freely exchanged, a couple will grow stronger and closer.

Jesus exchanged candid words with people he loved. When you look at the seven letters to the seven churches in Revelation 2 and 3, you see a gentle Savior saying some difficult things to the churches he loved enough to die for:

- The church at Ephesus: "Yet I hold this against you . . . " (2:4)
- The church at Smyrna: "Do not be afraid of what you are about to suffer . . ." (2:10)
- The church at Pergamum: "Nevertheless, I have a few things against you . . . " (2:14)
- The church in Thyatira: "Nevertheless, I have this against you . . . " (2:20)
- The church in Sardis: "Wake up!" (3:2)
- The church in Philadelphia: "Hold on to what you have . . . " (3:11)
- The church in Laodicea: "You are neither cold nor hot . . . " (3:15)

Jesus' gracious heart constrained him to address areas these churches needed to deal with. Yet each letter was a love letter—a call to something greater, higher, and eternally noble. In the same way, there are all kinds of issues that need to be addressed in marriage. Sometimes they're needs that come directly from the relationship. Others come from the way our spouse is dealing with people (perhaps your kids) or handling a certain challenge in life. Marriage needs to have a means by which we can speak into each other's lives with gracious candor.

Maintaining a Climate of Candor

The freedom to be candid is more than just the ability to speak what's on your heart to your spouse; it's also their freedom to tell you what's on their heart. This freedom to open your hearts to each other should be a light that's always green. We need to reflect Jesus' heart by allowing our spouse to feel they have ongoing permission to approach us with heavy issues on their heart—even if these heavy issues have to do with us.

What are the hours that God is available to process our hurts, frustrations, and fears? Nine to five? Monday, Wednesday, Friday, except holidays? Maybe just Sunday and high holy days? These are silly questions, aren't they? In the same way that God is always available to us, we need to give our spouse permission to speak up whenever they need to.

At the same time, this isn't license for a high controller or drama queen (or king) to feel like they can maintain an open-ended harangue or pick an inconvenient or inappropriate time for a discussion. Likewise, candor doesn't mean that every time one spouse wants to talk, the other spouse is required to have a full-disclosure, let's-roll-around-in-our-mess fest. Even God, with his Always Open sign, doesn't permit us to abuse the privilege. James 4:3 addresses the issue of coming to God with wrong attitudes: "When you ask, you do not receive, because you ask with wrong motives, that you may spend what you get on your pleasures."

All this said, God does indeed have an Always Open sign. He assumes an approachable posture that is saturated with grace. In Hebrews 4:16, the writer says, "Let us then approach the throne of grace with confidence, so that we may receive mercy and find grace to help us in our time of need." We have access to God's very throne room—his "throne of grace"—whenever we need it.

The reason our spouse needs to have this freedom with us is so we can keep bitterness from becoming a taproot in our relationship. Hebrews 12:15 says, "See to it that no one falls short of the grace of God and that no bitter root grows up to cause trouble and defile many."

In our role as parents, Darcy and I knew we would do and say things that could cause our kids to struggle with disappointment. We were two imperfect people trying to raise four imperfect kids. That's why we instituted "What's Your Beef?" nights. These were dinners, declared in advance, where the kids could voice any frustrations or embarrassments they'd had to process because of something Darcy and I had done or said. We qualified that this was about personal things we'd done—not their frustration with the fact that we expected them to get up each morning, go to school, do their homework, and be nice to each other. We were referring to infractions against their hearts that we might have done either deliberately or unwittingly.

For dinner, we'd fix each child their favorite entrée and then go around table and let each of them discuss any of these issues. All Darcy and I were allowed to do was apologize. We weren't allowed to put what we said or did in context or try to explain our bigger reasons. If we had done that, the kids would have seen that the game was fixed. Instead, we just apologized and asked for their forgiveness.

We did these dinners for two reasons: we didn't want our children having to balance a chip on their shoulder that we had put there, and we wanted them to know they had the freedom to talk candidly to us about *anything* that was bothering them . . . at any time. They didn't have to wait for a "What's Your Beef?" evening to clear the air with us. We also wanted them to know they truly had the freedom to talk with us about *anything*, whether it was about fears they had, temptations they were wrestling with, or sins they had committed. We gave them the freedom to be candid.

But It Takes Two to Be Candid

What's interesting is how easily Darcy and I were able to do this for our kids and how difficult it was for us to do it with each other. Candor is like the game of catch: it requires not only someone throwing something to us, but us catching it and throwing it back. I suppose this concept of catching and throwing could be seen in a negative light—if you've never played catch. We're not talking about chucking rocks at each other. We're talking about one of the greatest games of all time. Catch requires cooperation and a desire of each person to help the other person succeed. In a grace-filled marriage, spouses know they can vocalize their deep troubles or concerns graciously, and they are equally committed when they are the recipient to take the words to heart.

I think this calls for a shift in voice.

Darcy's Story

I've asked Tim to let me take over the keyboard again for a page or so. I want to weigh in with my story regarding the need for candor in a marriage. I had to learn the hard way what a wonderful gift this is to a marriage because candor was not part of my makeup when Tim and I got married. And when I saw what candor looked like, I didn't want it to be part of our ongoing relationship either. Let me explain why.

I grew up in a family of six children. As you can imagine, my parents worked very hard to provide for our large family. But all families have issues. Mine was no exception. For me, the problem was that my dad was a workaholic and chose to operate emotionally distanced from all of us. After I learned some of the dark secrets about my dad's childhood when I became an adult, his gruffness and harshness were explainable, even if they were never justified.

All six of us kids desperately wanted to gain his approval, and each of us, in our own way, used our natural strengths to strive for that blessing every child longs for from their father. I like things peaceful, and I like things perfect. So I tried very hard to minimize the tension between my father and me (read: never disagree or challenge misguided accusations). I also went the extra mile to make sure I did everything as well as possible.

To win my father's blessing, I tried my best to be perfect at the things I did. For those of you who grew up in an alcoholic home, you probably know this is a typical tactic children use in those homes—especially daughters. Although my father was never an abuser of alcohol, his obsession with his work created some of the same toxic dynamics for us kids. I was careful to steer clear of the things I knew I couldn't do at a high level of excellence. It's easy to look better than you actually are if you never step out of your comfort zone. Image control is so duplicitous!

I thought if I could just stand out in everything I did and cause no waves in the process, I might catch my dad's attention and maybe even get a nod of approval.

My father, who never used encouraging words when speaking to any of us kids, would nonetheless put us up on a pedestal and boast about his "trophy" family to his friends and colleagues. It was difficult to hear him brag about me to the people he worked with, when he would never speak words of appreciation to me directly. Rather than giving me a sense of approval, this insincere bragging made me want to be even more perfect.

Then I fell in love with Tim, the adventurer and risk taker. Tim naturally loved the things about me that I so carefully managed to do or present perfectly. But when we got married, he quickly found out that while I was well polished in some areas, I—like everyone else—had major gaps in my abilities and flaws in my attitudes.

When I was insensitive, acted unloving, or had a bad attitude—and he tried to discuss these things with me—I became defensive and stubborn. I did two things over and over: I threw the problem back on him as though it was all his fault, and I refused to admit that I had done anything wrong. *How could I be wrong?* I'd think. *I'm supposed to be perfect—and if I'm not perfect, then who am I?* His analysis and admonishment threatened the very core of how I had learned to define myself, as well as what I'd put in place to gain the approval of others.

So for many years of our marriage, instead of our being able to speak candidly to each other, I shut him off with self-righteousness and left him to work through his exasperation of knowing there was more to our disagreements than just his contribution to them.

Fortunately, Tim wasn't satisfied allowing this to continue as a way of life for us, and I didn't want it that way either. I was an heir of the gospel, of Jesus' work for me on the cross. The more I learned about what the grace of Calvary truly was, the more my heart yearned for it to redefine me. Additionally, God's grace continued to wash over me in the form of a grace-filled husband. I was able to find something in my marriage I never got to enjoy in my childhood. Tim began to show me that his love wasn't like what I thought my dad's love was—contingent on my behavior, my appearance, or my performance. He reminded me that everyone has flaws; we all get it wrong sometimes. His candor wasn't a brutal honesty that only pointed out my missteps and failures; it was a kind and gentle journey to the foot of the cross to remind me that Christ died for my mistakes and loved me in spite of who I was, not because of who I was. And because of this journey we've taken in our marriage, I have come to trust that Tim also loves me, even with all my imperfections.

Talk about freedom! I no longer have to keep up an unsustainable effort to reach the unattainable goal (perfection). And this freedom doesn't make me less focused on pleasing my husband; it makes me want to be even more of a loving wife. It's the same way with Christ. His forgiveness and love don't give us license to be selfish and do whatever we want; they compel us to love him more.

It's Tim Again

As you can see, both Darcy and I brought toxic issues to our marriage. We share that reality with every other couple who has ever exchanged vows. Just like you, we had a choice. We could let these issues rule our lives, define our partnership, and sully our love, or we could deal with them candidly, graciously, and with each other's best interests in mind.

If someone were to capture the essence of grace-filled love in a song, it would sound more melancholy than upbeat, more blues than pop. Yet the best love songs are the ones about real people working through real issues and real imperfections to arrive at a meaningful lyric and a memorable tune. A candid exchange of the deeper matters of the heart between a husband and wife—within a culture of grace—can mold love into something far more valuable than anything it could ever have gained otherwise.

God designed marriage to be a safe place to work through our personal junk. Whether we're giving or receiving, if we're willing to let the love that saved us from our sin be the love that guides us on our way, we can serve each other's best interests without turning these rough adjustments into war zones.

Before I leave this discussion on candor, I want to mention an overriding principle Darcy and I have learned that helps the process not only run more smoothly but reach a better conclusion more quickly. When you and your spouse are talking your way through tough issues, *the goal of the discussion should always be unity, never victory*. If you're committed to a grace-filled marriage, you should never be motivated by "winning" an argument.

There's a practical reason you don't want to make it your aim to win the arguments you have with your spouse. If you consistently win arguments with your mate, guess what you get to sleep with every night? A loser! And if your spouse loses often enough, they might start thinking they're a loser and acting like one.

Grace isn't about showing up the other person. Victory is about self. Unity is about relationship. When it's leading the way in difficult discussions, unity gets to enjoy its rightful place in our marriage because Christ enjoys his rightful place in our hearts.

The Freedom to Make Mistakes

This last dimension of grace is the hardest freedom for most people of faith to grant to their spouse. The reason it's so tough is because in marriage, we're no longer two but one. Our mistakes, whether past or present, affect both of us. Therefore, when our spouse really messes up, usually we have to pay a high personal price for their folly. Also, our spouse's gigantic sins are often directed *at* us. So we must absorb a double-barreled shot. It stands to reason that we have a difficult time approaching these infractions with a grace-filled attitude.

Darcy and I have met a lot of couples who desperately needed to give a spouse the freedom to make mistakes but chose other paths when faced with the hard realities of trying to love someone who has let them down. I'd like you to meet one such couple. Their names have been changed, but their story will serve us well when it comes to understanding what grace looks like when our spouse makes extremely poor choices.

If you were looking for a guy with all the qualities you'd want in the man who marries your daughter, Chad was your poster boy, with charm, brawn, and drive. Tracy was first-string varsity level too. They both had the intelligence, connections, and financial head start most would assume would make a marriage-made-in-heaven partnership. And they were both followers of Jesus. That's how they met—at church.

One more thing: They hadn't chosen to take the standard sexual route to their marital bed that today's culture encourages. Instead, both had decided to save the sexual part of their relationship for their wedding night. Because of it, they had one whoop-de-doo first night in their honeymoon suite. In fact, they had a whole week of them. All that week—sitting by the pool, taking walks on the beach, looking across candlelit meals at Tracy, and falling asleep with her spooned inside his arms—Chad couldn't believe this was really going to be his life.

What he didn't know was that it wasn't remotely close to the life he would have with Tracy. And I'm not referring to the adjustments all couples make when they come home from their honeymoon to the responsibility of married life. He was ready for that. What he wasn't ready for was Tracy's almost immediate decline in sexual desire. At first, he just figured it was the demands of their busy lifestyle. But when the frequency of intimacy shifted from a couple times a week to weekly to monthly to (within three years) only Valentine's Day and his birthday, he knew what he thought he had signed up for was something he might never have.

Which was when his mind and eyes started to drift.

Obviously, Chad and Tracy had talked about their lack of sexual intimacy. But the conversations left them both angry and sanctimonious about their indignation toward each other. She felt his expectations were selfish, that he should be more sensitive to her needs. He felt that the exact same argument could be used against her. The more he voiced his disappointment in their lack of intimacy, the less she felt like meeting him halfway. Discussions became arguments that became shouting matches that became days—and sometimes weeks—of avoiding any kind of meaningful conversation.

At the height of their frustrations, they did something that didn't help their situation at all—they shared their disappointments with close friends. When you're reacting emotionally and presenting a case from anger, it's impossible to be objective. But objectivity was never their goal. They wanted their friends to validate their reasons for being angry with each other. The way she framed him in her girlfriends' eyes left them to conclude that he was a sexually demanding, egotistical pervert. His friends were certain he married a woman who could make the iceberg that brought down the *Titanic* look like an ice cube by comparison.

Chad didn't know that Tracy had brought a secret to their wedding. She wasn't what she had advertised herself to be back when they met in church. It was a combination of preoccupied parents, the early arrival of the breast fairy, the interest of boys in general, and the interest of an adult man in particular. This man was a friend of the family who never forcefully molested her but became involved with her sexually while she was a minor. Legally, he could have been brought up on abuse and assault charges—and he should have been—but Tracy knew she had been a willing participant.

Who knows the ghosts that haunted this young girl? Regardless, she went from this man to others. But her sexual activity wasn't the standard stuff that many teenagers get involved in. Tracy called what she pursued nothing less than brazen promiscuity—awful things that she had done and that awful men had done to her.

Then two things happened that helped her change direction. Her family moved to a different state, and she heard the gospel. She put her faith in Christ's work for her on the cross, but unfortunately, she didn't put her faith in his *finished* work on her behalf. She accepted the part about Jesus coming to save her from hell and give her eternal life. But she didn't realize that he also came to free her from all the guilt and shame she had carried through her youth. He died so that she could gain a forgiveness that could put that stuff behind her forever.

She grew in her knowledge of God, but she never allowed Jesus to lift the burden of shame off her. It was in this corridor of time when she met Chad.

Many women in Tracy's shoes feel the repercussions of previous sexual experiences on their honeymoons. Right out of the blocks, they feel shame and guilt. And these feelings often ruin the show. Tracy had at least risen above that. She was hoping her marriage would heal the wounds that were still wide open in her heart. Instead, it just accentuated them. Her sexual encounters with Chad reminded her of those many times with so many other men. She was repelled by the memories. In other words, Satan was wearing her like a cheap suit.

Chad and Tracy's lack of sexual intimacy was complicated further when Tracy stopped exposing her naked body in front of Chad. In the early months of their marriage, she'd often jump in the shower with him and always dressed and undressed around him. Chad appreciated this part of his new life as a married man—especially married to such a beautiful woman as Tracy. But little by little, that, too, started to slip away from him. She'd shower with the bathroom door locked and get dressed after he had already headed to the kitchen for breakfast.

Chad had always thought, and even been taught, that one of the spiritual benefits of marriage for the man is that you don't need to worry about wanting to fixate on other women, or the beauty of some image in a magazine or online, because you'll have your bride's body to gaze on each day like a gift from God. Well, the curtain fell on that show just after its opening act. Years of longing, pleading, and fighting had magnified the urge that had been growing in him to see what the Internet had to offer. He succumbed. Pornography sunk its hooks deep within him.

In time, Tracy found out *his* secret. He was embarrassed and immediately took responsibility for this awful alley he had chosen to go down. What Tracy came back with was not a response of a grace-filled wife who was sad to see Satan trying to steal her husband's dignity and wreck their marriage. Hers was pure reaction— not untypical of the reaction of lots of women faced with the same dilemma with their husband. "I can't believe you'd do this to me! You should be so ashamed of yourself." (He was.) "It's disgusting.

You're disgusting! I want you to keep your sleazy hands off of me!"

Tracy's reaction involved disgracing him, punishing him, and isolating him from her (she made him move out). The ultimate humiliation for him was what she did to his reputation. She told the women in her Bible study (who, in turn, told their husbands), called her pastor about it, and then told her parents as well. He was utterly destroyed. She made absolutely sure there was nothing left of him.

Finally, they went to a counselor. In short order, this umpire of the soul rooted out Tracy's secret from the deep hole where she had buried it and brought it out into the light of transparency. Now it was Chad's opportunity to decide whether to respond or react. He took the low road. "You mean to tell me our sexual life has been held hostage all these years by some poor choices *you* made as a teenager? Let me make sure I'm getting this straight—all this time, I have been punished for someone *else's* crimes against you? Tracy, I was the one who stepped forward to love you. I was the one who believed in you. And all this time, my lying awake next to you for so many nights over so many years wondering what was wrong with me was simply because you'd rather hurt me than deal with *your* issue?" The initial exchange didn't go well.

There were many opportunities for Tracy to offer grace to Chad and for him to lavish grace on her. But because they were not committed to candor, they were held hostage by their secrets. And when the truth finally came out, they had no desire to be used by God to help each other process their setbacks and sins, so they denied that truth the power it had to set them free. As a result, they ended up as sock puppets to the enemy. What could have been radically different was denied because Chad and Tracy were unwilling to appropriate the same kindness, understanding, and forgiveness God had extended to them.

Chad and Tracy were nice folks when they started out. They genuinely loved each other and neither would have ever wished the misery they ultimately caused in the other's life. But because they didn't invite grace into their relationship, they became each other's greatest adversaries.

Sin through the Grace Lens

Sexual promiscuity is a toxic lifestyle choice. Pornography is a serious breach of the intimacy in a marriage. There's no question that what happens within these two worlds is not something anyone would want to treat lightly. But in all my years of working with couples within the family of faith, the more difficult issue is not how wretched the sinful traps are that people fall into, but how punitive the reaction is of believers close to these people who fall into these traps. I *assume* people are going to slip and fall hard on their faith journey. This isn't to trivialize the enormous impact of their sin or to absolve them of responsibility or consequences. But if anyone should understand how treacherous, cunning, and relentless the forces of evil are, it should be someone who has been rescued from evil's clutches by the gospel.

It's sad to see the level of punishment one believer will pour out on another once they've learned that they've been let down. It makes me wonder, "Do these people have any clue what Christ did for them at the cross?" The answer, obviously, is that if they do, it's either limited in scope or overshadowed by rage.

I can appreciate the reasons for hurt as well as anger. It hurts to find out your wife has been betraying your trust and punishing you because of something you had nothing to do with. I can appreciate the disappointment, embarrassment, and repulsion a woman must feel when she learns her husband has been sharing something with some phantom sex machine online that he was only to give her. If that's all we allow our hearts to feel, there are only going to be cold, maybe even heartless, reactions.

Double Vision

But how would Jesus look at these same scenarios? He'd see the sin. He'd feel the thorns, the spikes, and the spear that sin cost him. But he'd also see the person—he'd see Tracy, defined by her shame, locked down in her regret, and his heart would break for her. He'd see Chad, with all of his secrecy, disgrace, and embarrassment, and he'd pity him.

One of the ways to measure how effectively we grasp the magnitude of God's grace is this: When someone sins—and in particular, sins against us—what comes first to our mind? Is it anger? Maybe disappointment? Even more, thoughts of condemnation? Are we quick to start piling the rocks for the metaphorical stoning we think that person deserves? If these are the responses that surface first, most likely we have a restrictive view of God's grace. Even more, we have a very small understanding of what he did for us personally.

You may say, "Tim, these sins are direct hits on the spouse you're calling out. It's the innocent spouse who must bear so much of the shame and hurt. These are sins that were done against this spouse."

True. All of this is true. And if all we're dealing with here is right and wrong, guilt or innocence, then this conversation would be over. But that's not all we're dealing with. We're dealing with inherently valuable people who have lost their way, gotten sucked into Satan's muck, or have let their weaknesses get the best of them. It doesn't mean they aren't guilty. It doesn't mean there shouldn't be consequences. But is our response in any way aligned with the way Jesus processes these same crimes? He was the innocent victim of the full brunt of our sin too. But he chose not to leave us or forsake us in the midst of processing the pain of our sin against him.

Jesus seems to keep two things separate in his mind. On the one hand are the person's actions; on the other hand is the person. He maintains a righteous justice toward a person's actions while at the same time never letting go of holy mercy toward the person. He never lets the momentary infraction overshadow the value of the eternal soul who committed that sin.

The men who brought to Jesus the woman they'd caught committing adultery (John 8) were focused only on her sin, with no regard for her as a person. They wanted her killed and hoped to use the opportunity to embarrass Jesus. Her sin was all that was important to them. She, as an individual, meant nothing. Jesus, however, saw her through a completely different lens.

In John 4, Jesus' disciples got crossways with him when they discovered he had been sitting at a public well, exchanging recipes with a woman who had been married five times and was currently cohabitating with a man. Jesus wasn't focused on her poor choices or the wretched life they had created for her, but rather the fact that she urgently needed grace. He saw a woman in desperate need of living water.

It's hard to think of anything worse than betrayal. That's what Chad and Tracy were processing in their marriage. Jesus knew what that blade felt like coming into his back. He also knew what it felt like when the person holding the knife was one of his best friends,

Peter. But Jesus separated his attitude toward Peter's upcoming denial from his love for him as a dear friend and processed each one accordingly (Matthew 26:31–35; Luke 22:31).

A Lover's Eyes

I have a close friend who is an orthopedic surgeon as well as a wise follower of Jesus. We were talking about the tendency Christian couples have to lash out at each other's sin rather than extend God's grace to rescue their spouse from their sinful free fall. He said, "A hypochondriac is a person who thinks they're sick when they're not. A hypocrite is a person who thinks they're sinless when they're not."

We are more inclined to condemn when we've lost sight of the enormous forgiveness we've received from God. But we can rise above this in a grace-filled marriage. Darcy and I have found that our relationship is better when we preach the gospel to ourselves individually every day—when we remember the undeserved grace God has given us. It's much easier to look past the pointed edges of our spouse's sin—even with its personal cost to us—when we focus on their desperate need for rescue.

For Chad and Tracy, grace didn't fill their relationship instantly. They both had three big issues: their personal sin, their frustration with each other's sin, and their narrow view of grace. It was on this third issue that they camped first. Their counselor coached them on what lovers see when they view each other through the lens of God's grace. This helped them take the next step of accepting responsibility and God's forgiveness for their misdeeds. From there, the natural next step was to forgive each other. It's hard to forgive someone else when you've withheld forgiveness from yourself.

They also added another dimension to their recovery: they stopped viewing each other as an enemy. Chad and Tracy had chosen to marry each other because of the value, potential, and hope they saw in each other. None of that had changed; it just got covered over by layer upon layer of anger and disappointment. Fortunately, they finally recognized their real enemy. The power of darkness was trying to steal their love, destroy their sexual intimacy, and wipe out their marriage.

Tracy began to see Chad through a lens that wanted to protect him from pornography and encourage him as he waged war against its pull. They faced it as a team, but they weren't going to rely on just the commonsense steps that help minimize exposure. They wanted an inside-out, top-to-bottom victory over the influence of pornography. One way Tracy felt she could help Chad fight this battle was to make sure he wasn't going around sexually hungry.

Equally, Chad's heart ached for what Tracy had endured in her wayward teenage years. He identified with the desperate struggle she had borne for so long as a result of those years. They also took responsibility for the damage they had done to each other's reputation. Fortunately, they found out there were more grace-filled couples in their circle of friends than they realized—couples who were willing to join them in their fight against their real enemy. When Chad and Tracy decided to lock arms and fight their real enemy together with God's power—instead of donning their armor and beating up each other—God's grace rained down over them. He gave them a new love and a safer, clearer path to follow together, and ultimately, he restored the passion of their honeymoon bed.

The First Step

Before we lay this discussion to rest, I need to make clear that although grace needs to be the lens through which we view our spouse's sins, there is a need for genuine repentance on the part of the one who has failed. Repentance is the first step toward God and has to be a first step toward our spouse when we've let them down.

True repentance doesn't minimize the severity of sin, make excuses, or pass the buck. It stands up, speaks up, owns up, and then shuts up. It assumes there are consequences for actions and willingly steps forward to take its lumps. Anything short of this is just you or your spouse blowing smoke where the sun doesn't shine.

Without genuine repentance, the healing process can't truly begin. But even if one member of the wedding photo is resistant to God's convicting work, grace can still play a role in the relationship. The consequences might be tougher and restoration put on hold, but God is glorified when we fight for our marriage, pray like mad, and trust him to deal with our unrepentant spouse.

Some of you reading this carry some serious marital scars. Your spouse has done some things that have made it hard to believe there's any hope for happiness in the future. Or maybe it's you who has delivered the bigger blows to the relationship. If you listen to the voices riding the wind around you, they'd say, "Cut your losses and dump the dude (or dudette)." That's the easy way out. For some of you, because of things over which you have no control, it may be all you're left with. However, last time I checked, God is the God of miracles.

I can't speak for you, but I hate it when the forces of evil win. Jesus went to a lot of trouble to kick Satan's sorry rear at a crossroads outside of Jerusalem. He wanted the victory he scored to resonate down through the end of time. Let it echo in you. Trust him. Believe his promises. Let his Word lift you up. He's a bigger God than any mess you or your spouse could have made.

All My Love, Jesus

As we close this chapter, let's review where we've been. We learned that grace thrives in the heart of our spouse when we make it our priority to meet their need for a secure love, a significant purpose, and a strong hope. We can infuse the fresh air of grace into our marriage when we give our spouse the freedom to be different, vulnerable, candid, and to make mistakes. All of these are counterintuitive unless we've been transformed by God's grace. But if we have, he can make these freedoms part of the climate of our marriage.

I don't know what you're facing in your marriage. You may feel that the consequences of poor attitudes and dumb choices have thrown your hopes to the wind. They may be issues involving your kids, money, parents, sex, work, ex-spouses, church, or unfaithfulness. God's grace wants to help you navigate through it all. There's love and mercy waiting for you over the horizon in the safe harbor of God's peace. Don't let life's contrary winds determine your destination—like a wise sailor, tack right into the worst of them with God's strength and watch him pull you through to calmer seas and a secure harbor. And don't be surprised if during the worst of the storm—when it looks like you've absorbed so much of its fierceness that you're sure you're going to sink—you sense his presence nearby and hear his voice call from the middle of its wail, "Take courage! It is I. Don't be afraid" (Matthew 14:27).

Your marriage is too important. Your family is too important. *You're* too important. And God's glory is worth it all.

The Character of Grace

If you ever get a hankering to run a marathon, I suggest you check it off your list in your twenties instead of waiting until you're much older. I know. I ran my first one the year I turned fifty.

I realize that for many people, the idea of running 26.2 miles for no other reason than to say they did never crosses their minds. When you start talking about wanting to do such a thing, total strangers often feel compelled to put their hand on your forehead to see if, perhaps, you've taken ill.

The first inclination I had to run a marathon started to heat up in my midforties. Up to that point, the only reason I could think of for running that far was if someone was chasing me. But the idea nonetheless slipped into my mind, simmered for several years, and then started screaming like a teapot that had finally hit the magic temperature. I announced to Darcy and my kids at a dinner late one evening in December that I was going to run a marathon the next year. Five hands immediately went to my forehead.

I had decided that if I was going to do what had to be done to get ready, why not make sure there was a great destination waiting for me? It's hard to beat the Big Apple. The New York City Marathon is always the first Sunday in November. I had ten months to get ready.

Great Illustration Material

A lot of good things came out of my preparation for that marathon (and the three others I ran). But above all of these things, I discovered a great illustration of marriage. It's easy to think that marriage is a series of short, quick sprints over a long period of time. The rest of the time, we can just take it easy. The good parson tries to warn us to the contrary during our wedding ceremony with all that for-better-or-for-worse, in-sickness-and-in-health stuff. But, as I've said before, at the altar we're usually young, full of ourselves, and fairly ignorant about the bigger demands of life.

Yet if anything's a marathon, marriage sure is. It's a demanding, lifelong arrangement that serves up all kinds of reasons to slip off the course, call a cab, and give up. But like a grand marathon, marriage is a glorious event. The planners of the New York City Marathon made sure all of us had a wonderful highlight reel tucked away in our memories when we returned home. Before we began, Mayor Giuliani welcomed us at our staging area on Staten Island. After a rousing rendition of "The Star Spangled Banner" and the explosion of cannons, we were off . . . across the bridge and through the historic streets of Brooklyn and Queens, to the throngs waiting for us in Manhattan, up to and through the Bronx, reentering the city to the sweet sounds of soul music in Harlem, and finally slipping into Central Park for our last miles to the finish line at Tavern on the Green.

As amazing as some of these sites were, they still must play second fiddle to the highlights God has for all of us on our marriage marathons. That is, *if* we do what needs to be done to prepare ourselves for the race and then manage ourselves wisely along the way.

Grace-Filled Long-Distance Running

Which brings us full circle to our discussion of the role of God's grace in our marriage. Marriage is a protracted, often grueling, race. It has the potential to offer a great highlight reel, but you have to do some hard things to make sure you're smiling in the pictures. When I decided I wanted to finish the New York City Marathon, I had to face some harsh realities. The first one was that if I kept doing what I had been doing and then just showed up at starting time, I was doomed. There are people who assume they can do that. They're sitting in a bar watching the runners going by on the televised feed of the race and think, *I'm in better shape than they are. Next year, that's going to be me!* So they show up. A few even brag about all the sacrifices they didn't make and all the miles they didn't run. Some chide about the enviable finish times they're going to record. They're the ones you see throwing up off the Verrazano-Narrows Bridge into New York Harbor in the first few miles of the race. They're also the ones you see on the subways later in the day with their racing bib pinned to their shirt, but no finisher's medal hanging around their neck.

Just like marathons, grace-filled marriages require a commitment to sacrificial changes in your life. These are coupled with a resolve to maintain these commitments throughout the duration of your race—till death us do part. On January 1 of that marathon year, I had to make some hard choices. Obviously, I would have to put a lot more miles on my running shoes than ever. I started out conservatively with full knowledge I would have to radically increase the base amount of miles I ran each week as I got closer to the starting time. By the late summer months, I knew I'd have to set aside blocks of time for running the eighteen-, twenty-, and twenty-two-mile build-up runs on weekends. I also had to commit to guarding my rest and eating carefully. A new addition to my lifestyle would be all the running magazines and websites I had to read on a regular basis, as well as the runners I'd need to confer with during my preparation. These are the things you do if you want to *finish* a marathon.

Besides these things, I also had to resolve to resist all the things that would tempt me to fudge on any of those January 1 decisions—things like fatigue, darkness, rain, cold, heat, fever, head colds, or desserts.

Darcy made my goal a team effort. There were lots of things she had to coordinate with me to make sure I stayed on point: meals, schedule, and the application of a lot of ice before and after long runs. She even enlisted the kids to be at key points of those really long runs to cheer me on. Unfortunately, my kids also have a sick sense of humor. On one of my pass-bys, I could hear my oldest daughter, Karis, screaming, "Run, Forrest! Run!"

Darcy and I have been learning how to take the gracious love we received from Jesus at the cross and turn it into the modus operandi of our marriage. It's a grand plan that lets his truth guide us and his gracious heart temper us. A grace-filled marriage—where kindness, sacrifice, an outward focus, and selflessness dominate our relationship—sounds nice on paper. It's like the website for a marathon. Anything can be made to look good online. Turning it into a reality requires a lot more than idealistic images. Especially so when we get a good look at what a grace-filled marriage looks like lived out day after day . . . drenched in sweat.

That's what we've been doing in this book. We've discovered that grace takes the initiative to fill the tanks of our spouse's need for a *secure love,* a *significant purpose,* and a *strong hope.* One of the best ways to meet these needs is within a climate of grace. We learned that a grace-filled atmosphere in marriage assures our spouse the freedom to be *different, vulnerable, candid,* and to *make mistakes.* What we need now is a clear understanding of what is required to make these gracious commitments a way of life.

Character Muscles

Anyone who's gone to a gym knows our body is made up of muscle groups. A well-rounded workout makes sure that all the muscle groups are developed. That's what we want to do when it comes to developing the strength we need to run, as well as finish, our grace-filled marriage marathon well.

The third level of our grace-filled napkin strategy addresses the *character* that sustains our commitment to meeting each other's inner needs, maintaining a climate of grace, and living for something bigger and more important than ourselves (which we'll address in the next chapter). Good intentions cannot sustain these commitments. Nor can good wishes, good starts, or good gear. We need those hard-core, well-carved, and totally ripped character muscles that can serve us well when the course terrain turns mean, the cultural weather refuses to cooperate, and there are no people on those long, isolated stretches of the race to cheer us on.

Once again, I have good news. God hasn't made this impossible. If you're willing to focus on six character muscle groups as a couple, you'll have all you need to appropriate the power of God for the long haul. That's the interesting thing about how a relationship with God is played out. He's willing to carry us through the tougher stuff; otherwise, he expects us to develop the spit and determination required to keep us running steady and strong—right by his side. In 1 Corinthians 9:24, the apostle Paul reminds us, "Do you not know that in a race all the runners run, but only one gets the prize? Run in such a way as to get the prize." The "run in such a way" is referring to far more than style or speed. It encompasses all the determination, training, obedience, sacrifice, and attitude of a conscientious runner. In marriage, this is where grace-motivated character serves us so well.

There are six character muscles that will provide incredible sustainability for your marriage:

- Faith
- Integrity
- Poise
- Discipline
- Endurance
- Courage

Each muscle group is capable of enormous torque. But when spouses flex them as a combined effort—powered by the love of God and focused on living out God's gracious heart as a couple—there's no stopping us. When we're willing to make sure these character muscle groups are isolated and exercised, we get to run a much more meaningful—and enjoyable—marital marathon.

Pink Elephants

It's no secret that most people don't keep themselves in very good shape. The excuses stretch over the horizon. But whether we're physically fit or out of shape, they're both the result of choices we make. One might be the default choice of not choosing the other option, but it's still a choice. We can choose to get up with the alarm, lace on our running shoes, and take off into the early morning cold, or we can choose to hit the snooze button. Either way, we've made a choice. And with each option, there are either rewards or negative consequences. They, too, are the result of choices *we've* made. So when it comes to the shape we're in, unless there are clear medical, physiological, or psychological explanations, whatever we see in the mirror is usually the product of choices we've made.

In the same way, whether we exercise good character or bad, whatever shows up is a result of choices we've made. Good choices are usually harder to make but provide a greater payoff. Poor choices are usually easier to make but come with nasty price tags. Either way, it's our choice.

Since these are our choices, why not make good ones? In a grace-filled marriage, we take responsibility for our decisions and refuse to embrace the hogwash that would keep us from doing the sweaty, sacrificial things that grace often calls for.

In the Old Testament, Joshua was coming to the end of his days. He had loyally served Moses for forty years. Then he had served with distinction as general of Israel's army for another forty years. In that time, God's enemies had been dispatched, the promised land had been divided, and the people had settled down to their new Starbucks life. But Joshua could see the handwriting on the stucco. He realized that many of these people—who had been beneficiaries of God's unwavering grace for so long—had short memories. Already they had started to sample some of the wrongheaded thinking and misdirected worship of the people they had displaced. Joshua saw them making poor choices—choices with consequences. So he laid the options out in front of them:

> If serving the LORD seems undesirable to you, then choose for yourselves this day whom you will serve, whether the gods your ancestors served beyond the Euphrates, or the gods of the Amorites, in whose land you are living. But as for me and my household, we will serve the LORD. (Joshua 24:15)

As married people, we can choose the more difficult but highly rewarding route of exercising good character—or the easier but more highly priced route of rejecting God's will for us. Either way, we've made a choice. But if we want God's grace to fill our marriage, we've got to get serious about the sweaty effort required to turn these character muscles into a grace-filled six-pack! It's great if we choose to do this as a couple. But regardless, each of us needs to make a decision to do it individually.

Over the years I've noticed that when a couple has trouble, it is *always* because one or both spouses have chosen not to exercise one or more of these character muscles. Likewise, when couples maintain a steady pace, sustain strong momentum when life serves them a steep hill, and keep padding forward toward the finish line, *without fail*, I've noticed that they're flexing all six of these character muscles. Is that motivation enough for us to dive into this discussion? Let's isolate each character muscle group and give them a good workout.

The Character Muscle of Faith

Anytime you think the Bible is serving up vague notions, you need to turn to Hebrews 11:6: "Without faith it is impossible to please God, because anyone who comes to him must believe that he exists and that he rewards those who earnestly seek him."

There's a cause-effect dynamic between our willingness to operate with confidence in God's almighty power and the degree to which God lets us access his pleasure. God is a good steward of his divine assets. And like any good steward, he's careful to entrust them to people who will handle them responsibly. He makes it clear that if we want access to his pleasure—and the accompanying benefits (like the ability to tap into his grace)—we've got to *trust* him. It's even better when we trust him as a couple.

God wants us to trust him because of his track record (which we have from the Bible and history), what he's done for us personally (his loving, sacrificial death for us on the cross), and the way he continues to care for us. These are three *huge* reasons we shouldn't waver from our confidence in him, even when life comes at us hard. When we choose to trust God, he chooses to reward us—whether immediately or in the future, it's his call. But there is a clear consequence for *not* trusting him.

In Leviticus 26, God addresses the people of Israel, who had a ringside seat to observe his mighty hand. He's just delivered them from dreadful conditions against enormous odds. They've felt his presence and enjoyed his blessings. They have every reason to maintain faith in him. God tells them what he will do on their behalf if they continue to trust him (as demonstrated through obedience). The list of blessings is long and wonderful. But then he explains the obvious to them. What if, after all he's shown them, done for them, and all he's continuing to do, they choose not to trust and obey him? The list of consequences is equally long but awful.

There's an interesting statement right in the middle of these consequences that I think we need to take to heart both individually and as couples. God says that if you refuse to trust him, thereby disobeying him, "you will flee even when no one is pursuing you" (v. 17). That's another way of saying, "You'll be haunted by paranoia." When we refuse to trust God, in spite of all the evidence he's given us of his love, mercy, and power, our fears will take on Goliath proportions, even though no actual (or at least substantive) threat genuinely exists. One of the things that often stands out in people who refuse to trust God is how intimidated they are of things that, for the most part, are exaggerations of reality or complete figments of their imaginations. That's a consequence of not exercising faith. God is serious about how much he wants us to trust him!

So how do you know if you truly trust him? The answer to that question is best settled by a series of other questions:

- How do you process bad news?
- How do you behave in the midst of emergencies?
- Do you find yourself fretting about money, your health, aging, or unknowns?
- How much of your prayer life is about God clearing obstacles out of your way?
- Do you allow your past sins to limit you as an individual or to tamper with you as a couple?

I think it's obvious what the answers would sound like if you're not functioning in a state of faith. But how would a person who truly has confidence in God's power and grace answer these? How would you answer them if your answers represented the combined attitudes of your hearts as a couple? I think God's Word would direct the answers to sound something like this:

- How do you process bad news? *It depends. If it's bad news as a result of something stupid we've done, we try our best to be quick to repent and take our lumps. If it's just the typical bad news that goes with living on earth, it makes us sad and might even scare us some—but no one ever said we get to maintain a permanent address in Disneyland. We know God will sustain us regardless, so we choose to rest in him.*

- How do you behave in the midst of emergencies? *They immediately scare us. That's why they're called emergencies. But we know two things: they're now our emergencies that need to be faced head-on, and although they've caught us off guard, they're not a surprise to God. Even though we might be frightened by emergencies, threatened by the unknowns they create, or overwhelmed by the decisions we have to make, we know we worship a good God who has these chapters in our story completely under control. We know he'll lead us through them.*

- Do you find yourself fretting about money, your health, aging, or unknowns? *Only when those problems are because of something dumb we've done. Then we assume the fretting is God's conviction tugging at our hearts. If that's the case, we need to take that issue to him and seek his forgiveness. Otherwise, these things are the game-board pieces of life. God can use all of these for our good and his glory. Frankly, we see them as opportunities to enjoy a front-row seat to his sustaining grace.*

- How much of your prayer life is about God clearing obstacles out of your way? *That would ruin the fun! Prayer isn't about God making our life easy; it's about his Spirit strengthening us as his followers . . . whatever may come.*

- Do you allow your past sins to limit you as an individual or to tamper with you as a couple? *No. What sins? They got washed downstream in that flow of blood that poured from our Savior. How could we let something control us that no longer exists? If we do, we are giving Satan the high ground in our thinking. Obviously, our faith in Christ didn't give us amnesia. We haven't forgotten the awful things we did. In fact, they are an ongoing reminder of how much Christ loved us. Also, their memory gives us greater mercy for people who are still trapped in their sin. But do our past sins still wield a negative influence over us? No. The price paid for those sins was precious and expensive, but that price was also paid in full. We're not going to insult God, or his work on the cross, by giving our past folly power it no longer has.*

That's how unwavering faith in God thinks, talks, and acts.

The faith we represent as couples is not our individual faith quotients added together and divided by two. The strong faith of one spouse still gets God's attention—even if the other spouse has no clue or interest. Paul and Silas gave this assurance to the Philippian jailer when they said, "Believe in the Lord Jesus, and you will be saved—you and your household" (Acts 16:31). The faith of Abraham saved the lives of his nephew Lot and Lot's daughters (Genesis 18:23–33). Paul's faith saved the lives of everyone with him on his perilous voyage at sea (Acts 27:21–44).

I think of a precious lady named Ruth. When she married Don, her faith hadn't developed beyond her childhood decision. But she decided to get serious with Jesus early in their marriage. Don, however, had other ideas. He kept up his monthly dues with agnosticism while falling overboard into a sea of booze. Yet Ruth never gave up praying, trusting, and believing that God would reach her family, protect their kids, and bless her marriage. When Don was struggling with alcoholism, God protected his children from him. Here's the happy ending: Every child put their faith in the God. Don ultimately climbed on the wagon for good. And not only did Don come to know Jesus, but he also went on to become one of Christ's great advocates. If I were to isolate Don's most outstanding feature as a follower of Christ, it would be his unwavering faith. He learned it from his wife.

It's nice if we exercise the faith muscle group as a couple, but the important thing is that it's exercised by *you*. God spent many occasions in the Bible saying, "Don't be afraid." There's a reason he said that. It's because, regardless of how bad, bleak, cold, or nasty things may appear, he's got *everything* under control. And when we choose to rest in that reality—pursuing him spiritually all the way—he loves to reward our faith. His primary reward is a peace that passes all understanding deep within our hearts.

If you want to have a grace-filled marriage, go to God's gym every day and work out your faith muscle.

The Character Muscle of Integrity

The push-pull our culture presents in the area of integrity is interesting. On the one hand, our society assumes—and sometimes even encourages—cut corners, cooked books, and self-protection. Reality shows are made out of these things. On the other hand, if you get caught, this same culture often takes delight in wiping you out. If that isn't proof of what the Bible says about Satan using culture to do his bidding (Ephesians 2:2), I don't know what is.

We also live in a world that is often tough on people who choose to do the right thing. Years ago, when Darcy and I were a young couple, we learned of another couple our age that was experiencing a professional crisis. The husband was in sales. Part of his job required him to travel and entertain clients as guests of his company. The unspoken tradition within the sales department was that the expense reports from these outings were excellent ways to pocket a lot of extra (yet unearned) money. The sales supervisors turned a blind eye to this practice because it was what they also had done when they were part of the sales team.

This young man always turned in accurate—to the penny—expense reports. But the difference between his and everyone else's showed a night and day contrast. His supervisor pulled him aside and explained the gentlemen's agreement that this particular department operated under. But the young salesman responded that it was out of the question. How could he present a falsified report? His supervisor thought him crazy and urged him to change his report. He refused.

Report after report went up through the chain to the financial department. The contrast caught a director's notice, enough so that he started to investigate the accuracy of this young man's expense reports as well as his comrades' padded ones. It became obvious that the sales team—with the exception of this young man—had been fleecing the company. New standards and systems were put in place, and then came the reprisals. Our friend became a pariah among his fellow salesmen. His punishment not only came from them but from his supervisor as well. The warm prospects that were normally supplied by his supervisor suddenly turned ice cold. Appointments were dropped from or added to his schedule without his knowledge to make him look incompetent. Even some of his sales contracts got lost or tampered with. The people he worked closest with did everything they could to get this young man fired or get him to quit—all because he chose to do what God expected him to do.

His own father-in-law thought he should stop all of this "honesty is the best policy" nonsense and play by the unwritten rules. But his wife stuck by his side, in support of his convictions and with full knowledge of what those convictions were costing them in income. She'd kiss him good-bye each morning and whisper in his ear, "I believe in you." This couple lost real money. They endured real sacrifice for a long time. But they stayed true to their convictions. They were people of integrity.

This was years ago. That young man is much older. He still works for that same company, but he's the CEO now. He makes more money annually than he did during his best five years as a sales rep put together. Doing the right thing doesn't always leave us at the top of the heap. That's not why we should do the right thing. Yet when we choose integrity, it's another way that the love God showed for us on the cross is given back to him in obedience.

If we want to receive God's blessing as well as enjoy his protection, we must have true content to our character. We need undaunted moral fiber driven by uncompromised moral convictions.

Moral convictions give life passion and purpose. That's why grace-filled couples don't tolerate a finders-keepers, losers-weepers attitude. They pay their fair share through life—and then some. Their taxes are accurate. Their word is trustworthy. When they mess up, they take responsibility. It might sound like a harder road than the convenient, self-serving path our culture encourages a couple to take, but there's an upside. Couples of integrity sleep better at night, their family doesn't have to keep a catalog of their deceptions, they never need to look over their shoulder, and they get to be daily recipients of God's favor. Psalm 101:2 says, "I will be careful to lead a blameless life. . . . I will conduct the affairs of my house with a blameless heart." And even when no one is actually watching us, Psalm 119:54 reminds us that people of integrity are known for the motto, "Your decrees are the theme of my song wherever I lodge."

God can entrust trustworthy people with his peace. You may not progress as fast as those who take moral shortcuts, but you'll be standing strong long after they've fallen away.

Possibly this section touched a nerve. Discomfort or embarrassment is often the ring from God's phone trying to get our attention. If we want his grace to be a regular part of our life, then on occasions like this, it's best to answer that phone call . . . and repent.

The Character Muscle of Poise

If we were looking for something to represent one of the biggest roles God's grace plays in our life, I think it would be a carpenter's level. When we travel close to God's heart, he keeps us from getting out of balance. I had a wonderful professor in seminary named Dr.

Howard Hendricks. He used to say, "Most people's lives aren't lived in balance. They just occasionally appear that way in those brief moments when they pass through the middle going from one extreme to the other."

It's easy to see how we could end up that way. We're carpet-bombed by messages that taunt us toward extremes in our purchases, opinions, politics, lifestyles, causes, theology, and preferences—just to name a few.

Regarding this poise muscle group that helps us maintain moral, spiritual, relational, physical, emotional, social, theological, and intellectual equilibrium, King Solomon said, "Do not be overrighteous, neither be overwise—why destroy yourself? Do not be overwicked, and do not be a fool—why die before your time? It is good to grasp the one and not let go of the other. Whoever fears God will avoid all extremes" (Ecclesiastes 7:16–18)

Earlier in Ecclesiastes, Solomon said, "There's a time for everything" (3:1), and then he went on to list fourteen contrasts (Ecclesiastes 3:2–8). Among them are:

- A time to tear down and a time to build up
- A time to cry and a time to laugh
- A time to mourn our losses and a time to party
- A time to embrace and a time to hold back
- A time to search and a time to give up
- A time to be silent and a time to speak up
- A time for war and a time for peace

In the context of our discussion on grace and the character muscles of poise, these passages beg a few questions: How do we know what time it is? How do we know we're moving toward an extreme? How do we know which option to embrace and to what degree? That's where God's grace comes to our rescue. God's grace is his heartbeat. It's the epicenter of his attitude regarding anything. And the best option is the one that most aligns with God's love expressed on Calvary. Anything we're doing becomes an extreme when it doesn't serve the highest and best interests of God's Calvary-type love.

I realize that's pretty abstract, but perhaps that's what God was talking about when, through the apostle Paul, he said, "We live by faith, not by sight" (2 Corinthians 5:7). Discussing the freedom we enjoy as recipients of the gospel, Paul also remarked, "'I have the right to do anything,' . . . but not everything is beneficial. 'I have the right to do anything'—but not everything is constructive" (1 Corinthians 10:23). Earlier in this same New Testament letter, Paul noted, "I will not be mastered by anything" (6:12).

God's grace keeps us from being mastered by anything other than him. We can get out of whack when we're mastered by our money, our status, our looks, our sex life, our theological elitism, our causes, our relationships, even our commitment to serving in our church. Over the years, I've had to help people who overvolunteer at their church to the harm of their marriage—all because they were trying to fill a void in their view of themselves. If we do good things for the wrong reasons, we're going to have bad outcomes.

If you'd like a working definition of *poise* to give you direction, try this: *poise is a keen spiritual sense of what is appropriate.* I know a marine sergeant who wishes she had learned this principle sooner.

My travels once took me to the Officer Candidate School at Marine Corps Base Quantico (Virginia). Among other things, I was invited to observe morning PT (physical training). There's a reason the marines discourage pushovers from stopping by their recruiting offices. It starts with their definition of *morning*, which is a couple of hours before most people think it starts. Another reason they suggest wussies need not apply has to do with what the Marine Corps considers "physical training." A typical marine burns more calories before breakfast than most people expend in a couple of days. I was transfixed.

On this occasion, the candidates formed on the O-course (obstacle course) at what I'd call zero dark early. There were several ropes suspended from logs that stretched across the O-course. These ropes were forty feet from deck to beam. The candidates wore shorts, T-shirts, and running shoes. The sergeants (staff, gunnery, and first) had on their standard green (at that time) utilities, starched and crisp, with combat boots and campaign covers. These sergeants were gentlemen marines who knew about fifty ways to help you meet your Maker. But in this group, there was also one marine gentlewoman. Though she wore the same uniform, she stood in stark contrast to other sergeants. Her gender obviously created part of the distinction, but the biggest difference was her size. She was what most would call "petite." But if you think that somehow diminished her capacity to kick your booty, you would be mistaken.

It's not uncommon for PT to last up to two hours. Although I didn't observe their whole workout, I was there to watch a good part of the beginning. Apparently, the petite sergeant was responsible for that morning's sequence of drills. She decided to get in a position where she could easily be seen as well as bark instructions to the candidates.

Sergeant Petite walked over to one of the ropes in the center of the O-course, got a good grip, and then pulled herself up by her hands to about two-thirds of its height. She positioned herself in a kind of relaxed posture with one leg looped through the line and then proceeded to call out what she wanted the candidates to do.

Sergeant Petite was still up there leading PT, holding on to the rope with just her hands, when I left a *half an hour later*!

Later that morning, I was in the barracks that housed both the candidates and the offices of the sergeants. It was here where I got to meet Sergeant Petite one-on-one. She was a pleasant lady, with a genuine smile and dry wit. We talked briefly about her work. I told her if she needed any tips on climbing ropes and hanging around on them for days on end, to let me know. She rolled her eyes. She knew that I was a Christian advocate for the family. Although I was fascinated by what she did, I was also curious about her as a person. There was a small framed picture on her desk of a girl—maybe five or six years old—who looked like a miniature clone of her. I inquired.

That's when I got a peek into a backroom of Sergeant Petite's heart. I soon learned she was divorced and raising her daughter with sole custody. I asked a couple of questions; she gave straightforward answers. And then Sergeant Petite did something I didn't think she was capable of doing—at least not around a civilian like me. She let a tear slip from one of her dark eyes and run down to her chin. She admitted, "I did something the Corps never asked or ever wanted me to do . . . I loved it too much."

She explained that they wanted her to love her Corps, of course, but never so much that it distorted the rest of the priorities in her life. "I mean," she said, "we all knew going in that the military is hard on marriages. But lots of vocations are. I can't blame what happened to my husband and me on my job. I simply let it consume me. Tim, I let myself believe that nothing and no one—not my husband, not my daughter . . . not even God—was more important to me than this." She waved both hands broadly, as though the Marine Corps encompassed not only the barracks we were standing in but the entire universe.

She continued, "My husband didn't stand a chance. I *really* hurt that man. Once I realized how foolish I was, I tried desperately to win him back. But . . . he left." She looked down for a moment. "I'm sure," she said, "you've heard the expression 'Once a marine, always a marine.'" I nodded. "It's true, and I'm proud of it. But I stood beside a great man at the base chapel many years ago and basically said, 'Once your wife, always your wife.' I could have loved both in balance. But I overloved my Marine Corps." She looked down at the picture on her desk. "Now it's just me and my daughter."

"And the Marine Corps," I added.

"No. Just me and her. We're the family. One of the officers—who should be doing what you do—said that I had let the Corps into the part of my heart God had meant for me to keep reserved for my husband. I'd also let it into the part I was supposed to keep reserved for him." She pointed and looked upward. "I'm working at shoring up things with God." She smiled. Then she said, "And I've even cleared the Marine Corps out of that part of my heart that was supposed to be my husband's, in case he ever wants to come back. But I'm pretty sure it's too late."

Poise is a keen sense of the appropriate. A heart guided by God's grace helps us keep the different parts of our life in balance. When that happens, we can bring much more to the other demands in our life. Grace wants to give our marriage equilibrium and plenty of relational oxygen. Couples who want to enjoy a grace-filled relationship make sure their poise muscle group is always kept well exercised and in tiptop shape.

The Character Muscle of Discipline

In the character muscle group of discipline, we're not talking about the discipline that comes our way because of wrong choices. We're talking about the things we do that allow us to avoid having to *be* disciplined.

The best way to understand the power behind discipline is to look at its synonyms: self-control, order, obedience, restraint, and confinement. All of these words define the heart of a grace-filled couple. In a world that touts its no-boundaries, everything-goes philosophies, we need to take our cues from God. That's because God has given us strengths as individuals and strengths as couples. But we can't maximize these strengths without discipline.

A great analogy would be the rails of a train. When you see a freight train pass by, it's overwhelming to try to calculate the sheer tonnage of goods and materials it is moving—sometimes at breakneck speed—from coast to coast. But all that power is confined to wherever the tracks are laid. As long as the train stays on those tracks, it exercises enormous power. But should it ever leave those tracks, it is forever known by a different name: a train wreck.

Discipline is what we apply to our strengths (like train tracks) to maximize their potential. Name any asset God has entrusted to your care as a couple, and you can imagine what a train wreck it can become if that asset isn't kept within the confines designed to give it maximum potential. How much do we have as assets? Let me count the ways . . . our time, energy, enthusiasm, bodies (as gifts to each other), money, curiosity, a sense of caution, a sense of adventure, trust, insight, children—and we're just getting warmed up!

There's a word that motivates disciplined people but comes off as an insult to undisciplined people: *lazy*. When God's grace has transformed our heart, we are motivated to maximize all the good things he's given us to work with. But when we surrender to our spiritual and relational sluggish side, the road less traveled tends to become the road never taken.

Spiritually disciplined couples do three things: they *delay gratification* because of *advanced decision making* in order to stay on target toward a *focused goal*. Listen to this:

> Everyone who competes in the games goes into strict training. They do it to get a crown that will not last, but we do it to get a crown that will last forever [a focused goal]. Therefore I do not run like someone running aimlessly [advanced decision making]; I do not fight like a boxer beating the air. No, I strike a blow to my body and make it my slave [delayed gratification] so that after I have preached to others, I myself will not be disqualified for the prize. (1 Corinthians 9:25–27)

When the love of God we received through the sacrifice of Jesus overflows in our hearts. . . .

- the priorities of our *callings* as couples don't get overshadowed,
- our *convictions* ramp up in intensity, and
- our harnessed *capabilities* are seen as opportunities to demonstrate our love for God and our commitment to each other.

If we want to run a steady marital marathon, we need to make sure we're working out our discipline muscles.

The Character Muscle of Endurance

In a marathon—especially a big-town event like the New York City Marathon—the runners are not only the main participants, but they're a big part of the color and fun of the event. Running groups often wear matching jerseys, individuals put funny statements on their shirts, and many don costumes. I saw runners dressed like Batman, Abraham Lincoln, the Statue of Liberty, and a bearded guy in a fairy suit complete with tutu, wings, and a magic wand.

But there were two people who grabbed my attention out of the group I had taken off with. They were a cute young couple who had gotten married in the staging area just before the start of the race. Apparently, they'd brought along someone who could make it legal, and along with a couple of friends as witnesses, they had gotten married near the edge of Fort Wadsworth, where the race begins. I'd seen them while I was stretching out nearby. He wore one of those tuxedo T-shirts, and she had on a veil—which she wore throughout the race—shoes decorated accordingly, and a bouquet.

We were in the same group as we took off. We maintained a similar pace throughout the race, with them getting out ahead of me, and then me sometimes passing them. The first time I passed them was in Queens. They had pulled over to the side of the course, and he was throwing up. Apparently, he had toasted his wedding a bit too much. He was bent over, and she was gently patting him on the back. *Isn't that nice?* I thought. *It's a great illustration of love in a marriage.* They caught up and passed me (remember they were young). I didn't see them again until about a mile into Central Park. She was sitting on the sidewalk holding up one of her legs with her shoe off as he tended to her heel. Blisters. *Another great illustration,* I thought.

At one point in the race, he needs her, and at another point, she needs him. Endurance is being there for each other throughout the race, so you can both cross the finish line.

Many things about marriage remind us of the need for endurance. We must be serious about continuing all the way to the end because of all the things we encounter along the way that incline us to quit. We've talked about many of them in this book. It is the rare couple who hasn't occasionally wondered if the finish line is worth all we have to go through to get there. But it is. One very encouraging passage from the Bible says this: "May the God who gives endurance and encouragement give you the same attitude of mind toward each other that Christ Jesus had, so that with one mind and one voice you may glorify the God and Father of our Lord Jesus Christ" (Romans 15:5–6).

God's Spirit empowers us as his grace keeps us padding forward through the good, the bad, and the revolting sections of the course before us. I sometimes wonder if the writer of the book of Hebrews had participated in marathons:

> Since we are surrounded by such a great cloud of witnesses, let us throw off everything that hinders and the sin that so easily entangles. And let us run with perseverance the race marked out for us, fixing our eyes on Jesus, the pioneer and perfecter of faith. For the joy set before him he endured the cross, scorning its shame, and sat down at the right hand of the throne of God. Consider him who endured such opposition from sinners, so that you will not grow weary and lose heart. (Hebrews 12:1–3)

It's easier to endure if we . . .

- keep in mind there are people depending on us (a great cloud of witnesses),
- keep ourselves unencumbered from foolishness (sin that so easily entangles us),
- resist veering off the course God has laid out (the race marked out before us), and
- keep our eyes on the finish line (fix our eyes on Jesus).

That extra *oomph* we need, that pep talk, that spouse pulling us up from the sideline and urging us forward is the grace of God. Look to whom the writer points to as the motivation for continuing, and what he explains as the reason for finishing our marital marathon: Jesus . . . and the cross. He says, "Fixing our eyes on Jesus . . . for the joy set before him he endured the cross . . . so that you will not grow weary and lose heart." Our power to endure is found in the gracious work of Jesus on our behalf. When we let his grace transform our hearts, that grace will serve us well, especially when we face the reasons that many use as excuses for giving up. And the more we endure, the greater our resolve to get to the finish line.

Take comfort in this: "We also glory in our sufferings, because we know that suffering produces perseverance; perseverance, character; and character, hope. And hope does not put us to shame, because God's love has been poured out into our hearts through the Holy Spirit, who has been given to us" (Romans 5:3–5).

Grace-filled couples who want to finish the race make sure they keep their endurance muscles ripped.

The Character Muscle of Courage

Big-city marathons staged on a crisp autumn day with a cast of thousands is one thing; taking on the long and often lonely road of a marital marathon, with just the two of you, is a different matter. Before you reach the finish line, things are going to cross your path that will frighten you beyond your imagination. First Corinthians 15:58 reminds us, "My dear brothers and sisters, stand firm. Let nothing move you. Always give yourselves fully to the work of the Lord, because you know that your labor in the Lord is not in vain."

God knows we're going to face things that frighten us, but he promises to give us all we need to overcome. You've heard the expression "fighting fire with fire"? It's true. And it works for fear too. Over the years, Darcy and I have learned that the only thing we need to face any fear is *a greater fear*. Sound crazy? Actually, it's straight from the Bible. We've learned that there is one fear that helps us rise above all others—the fear of God. Rumor has it that it's where the true wisdom for taking on life actually begins (Psalm 111:10). King David said, "When I am afraid, I put my trust in you" (Psalm 56:3).

Years ago, Darcy and I were in London. In one of the two main cathedrals, I'd read an epitaph on one of the many grave markers that I felt summarized the heart of a courageous person. I wrote it down. However, after I got home, I couldn't remember whether it was St. Paul's Cathedral or Westminster Abbey where I had seen it. Recently, we were over there again, and I tracked it down. It's in Westminster, the main nave, on the south aisle just to the right of the arch leading to the cloister. The man's name was Lord Lawrence. He was born in 1811 and died in 1879. He was a great man and lived an extraordinary life. Perhaps the reason is summarized in the words they carved for his epitaph: "He feared man so little, because he feared God so much."

We started this chapter talking about faith and ended by discussing courage. They're like the primary core muscles that make the other four muscle groups work even better. We said earlier that we make choices. On the one hand, we can choose a marriage that exudes a contagious faith, consistent integrity, practical poise, personal discipline, steadfast endurance, and inspirational courage. To have these, we've got to go to God's gym on a regular basis. Or we can make the decision not to exercise these muscles. We can calculate the effort and say, "The spiritual sweat required just isn't worth it." But it's still a choice. If we choose not to exercise these character muscles, we shouldn't be surprised that our marriage is badgered by uncertainty, we don't have a reliable reputation, we're at the mercy of life's extremes, most of everything that matters is out of whack, we're known as quitters, and we spend a lot of time feeling anxious and afraid.

The Finish Line

I was about fifty feet beyond the finish line, sitting on a curb eating an apple after I had completed the New York City Marathon. From where I sat, I could see the steady stream of runners reaching the goal. Darcy was waiting somewhere out on Central Park West for me, but that seemed like another marathon away. I'd have to talk my exhausted body into going to find her among the masses. Meanwhile, I needed some nourishment, so I thought I'd sit there for a while and savor the last moments of an amazing experience.

I could see through the finishing gate and down the lane to the runners still making their way. And then I saw *them*, about a hundred yards off in the distance. It was the newlyweds. They didn't have that lilt in their step or dance in their stride they had when I saw them take off at the starting line. They were covered with the dirt and sweat of more than twenty-six miles of work, setbacks, and pain. But there they were making their way to the end. Except they weren't side by side anymore. He was carrying her on his back. Apparently the blisters were simply too much. But rather than not finishing, or finishing without her, he had picked her up so they could finish what they started together. Her arms were around his shoulders and pressed against his sweaty tuxedo T-shirt. Her head bobbed next to his. She still had on her veil and was gripping her drooping flowers in her hand. But there they were.

I watched them all the way to the finish. When he took that last step across the finish line with his new bride, he quickly made his way to their right to avoid the incoming runners. Once clear, they fell into a heap in the grass just off the sidewalk. They just laid there in each other's arms while race officials covered them with race blankets, slipped their medals over their heads, and checked to make sure they were all right.

I finished my apple, sat there for a while enjoying the moment, and then pulled my body up. My leg muscles were tight, and I knew I still had a ways to go before I found Darcy. But I had to take one last look. I stiff-legged it back toward the finish line, against the flow of the incoming runners walking off their big accomplishments . . . and there they were. At first I thought they'd fallen asleep. But they were just lying there holding each other close. They both had that look of contented exhaustion—the kind a married couple gets when they make up their mind they're going to finish what they started regardless of what life brings their way.

I headed on to find Darcy, thinking, *Those kids are going to do just fine.*

——

CHAPTER 10

The Heart Qualities of Grace

—

As parties go, this one was particularly extravagant.

We were staying with friends. This party was an annual gala that had become a tradition for them. We told them we were fine with staying home, but our friends wouldn't hear of it. That's how Darcy and I found ourselves at a highbrow social wingding crowded with people neither of us knew.

After we cleared the front door and said hello to the hosts, Darcy took off with our friends to see something they wanted to show her, and I was left standing in a big room of strangers who were already grouped in animated conversations with each other. There was one couple standing by themselves over by the baby grand piano. I figured, *Okay, let's get this party started.*

She was a beauty queen. She told me . . . several times. Her friend was a heavy drinker. He never mentioned it, but I could count. What I figured would be a cordial meet and greet turned into a lengthy hostage situation.

My new friend hadn't won the Big One yet, but she was certain it was just a matter of time. The guy with her nodded his agreement and took another sip of his scotch. There was a preliminary pageant coming up that she figured she had a lock on. I had no idea what she was talking about, but she filled me in on the costumes, the backstage mayhem, the politics behind the judging, and the inside skinny on talent. I'd hoped I would die without ever knowing any of this stuff. She said that when she first started, her talent was cheerleading. But she switched to singing and dancing. I glanced nervously at the piano we were standing next to.

Oh, did I mention that Miss Congeniality was seventy-eight years old? At first I thought this was just some harmless senior citizen's thing and figured, *Good for her. She's having fun.* But as she kept talking, I realized this was not only the focus of her present life, but it had been the singular focus of her life since she was in college. She'd been participating in beauty competitions for almost sixty years! I asked about her children and grandchildren. She said something about having some but went right back to describing her life in front of the footlights. I asked her companion, who turned out to be her husband, about their kids and grandkids. He mumbled something and then waved to a waitress and pointed to his drink for a refill. I spent the bulk of that evening listening to this lady talk about herself, while watching her husband get inebriated. Neither of them questioned me about a single detail of my life. But, as you can see, when I finally excused myself and walked away, I could write a book on them.

The Focus of Our Life

Whether we like to admit it or not, every married couple's relationship is defined by something. That something will determine the color, flavor, texture, melody, and scent of the love in our marriage. Since the overarching focus of our married lives has the final say on how we play out our promises to each other, it's vital that we aim high.

Our discussion in this book has been addressing a simple thought: What if our relationship within our marriage was defined by the same thing God defines his relationship with his spouse—his grace? After we established why a grace-filled marriage is profound, we've been trying to get our head and heart around what God's grace actually looks like played out in the trenches of our daily lives as couples.

We've learned about inner needs, freedoms, and character muscles that enable us to bring the best out in each other. The last dimension of God's applied grace has to do with where we're aiming our marriage. Every marriage is aimed somewhere even if that somewhere is nowhere. Since it's not a case of *if* we're aiming our marriage, but *where*, why not aim it at something bigger than ourselves?

Before we look at where Jesus suggests we direct our attention, let's look at a handful of the usual subjects that married people choose. You might find yourself, or your marriage, hanging out among them.

A Reason to Get Up Each Day

When we get up every morning, something is framing the bigger picture of what we hope to accomplish. We all live with agendas. And most of us know what it's like when our schedule is determined by a lot of people other than ourselves. On top of this, there are items on to-do lists that need to be scratched off, kids with inexhaustible needs, employers who expect us to earn our paycheck, and many other demands that make up a busy day. But these aren't the things I'm referring to. These are the standard features of daily life that simply *have* to be done. What I'm referring to are those bigger aspirations that hang like curtains in the back of our thinking.

These always-there aspirations tend to hold the attention of our heart most of the time.

Success Goals

Some people get up, and the thing that most occupies their thinking is, *How can I make more money today?* They may be good at making money or merely wish they were. But whatever money they have isn't enough. There's always room in their bank account for more. Sometimes this driving focus is fueled by money they've lost. Regardless, these are people who think a lot about *wealth*.

Some people get up, and the thing that most occupies their thinking is, *How can I feel better about how I look today?* These folks either like the image staring back at them in the mirror or want to do something to improve that reflection. These people are usually good shoppers. It's a worldview enamored by *beauty* and the benefits that tend to come with it.

Some people get up, and the thing that most occupies their thinking is, *How do I expand my sphere of influence today?* They'd rather lead than follow. But it's more than that. They *need* to lead. But it's even more than that. They want to have control over as many of the variables of their life and the lives of people around them as possible. These are people who think a lot about *power*.

And then there are other people who get up, and the thing that most occupies their thinking is, *How do I get noticed more today?* They feel the world would be a better place if more people knew them on a first-name basis. It's not so much that they want to know these people personally as it is the satisfaction they gain by being known on a grander scale. When it's all said and done, what preoccupies their minds is their burning need for *fame*.

Wealth, beauty, power, and fame may not be the things that gnaw away at you as you go through your day, but they're the four horsemen of the apocalypse as far as our culture goes. A lot of husbands and wives wake up next to people who exist to have at least one of these superficial dreams filled in their lives.

But let's be fair. Sometimes these things occupy people's minds because it's part of their makeup. I'd even go so far as to say that it may point to some God-given gifts. God clearly gives some people a sixth sense of how to make money. There's nothing wrong with that. And if it's handled properly, this gift will hopefully benefit a lot more folks than just themselves. And what's wrong with trying to put your best foot or best face forward? Folks with aesthetic judgment bless us all with their art, design, color palettes, and eye for improvement. As long as they can still love the rest of us, everybody benefits. Some people are not only great leaders but popular ones too. People would prefer these leaders steering their destiny. Someone will always have power. If these people can do it well, why not them? And some people are well known simply because of something extraordinary they've done or something huge they presently do. They didn't necessarily seek fame; it found them.

The best way to know whether God is behind a person's wealth, beauty, power, or fame is simple: Did they set out or need to become wealthy, to be known for their looks, to take over as much of their sphere of influence as they could, or to become a household name? If so, then most likely, God wasn't behind those efforts. Their wealth, beauty, power, and fame were the result of their own fleshly endeavors. Generally, these self-directed efforts seldom enjoy happy endings. On the other hand, if wealth, beauty, power, or fame came as a result of their simply playing their assigned position in life carefully, without needing any of these outcomes, then most likely these are the results of their being who they were created to be.

But as I said, our culture worships these four things. Many married couples miss enjoying a greater and deeper purpose because one or more of these kick-you-out-of-bed-in-the-morning goals own their soul. But even more, many married couples miss the depth and passion of their intimate love for each other because one or more of these things have upstaged it.

Noble Goals

Some people get up, and the thing that most occupies their thinking is, *How can I better serve my family today?* They love their role as husbands, wives, parents, or grandparents. These are people who have a knack at good family dynamics or want to develop some. They *need* to have a family around them to complete their sense of happiness. That's fine as long as everyone cooperates. But seldom is it that everyone cooperates.

Some people get up, and the thing that most occupies their thinking is, *How can I do more for the poor and helpless?* Food, water, clothing, shelter, mercy, opportunity, and fairness are huge priorities for them because looking out for the downtrodden is a huge priority for them.

Some people get up, and the thing that most occupies their thinking is, *How can I make the world a better place?* These people are driven by a mighty cause. It might be the environment, politics, freedom, or human rights. They tend to think nationally or even globally. Their cause is never far away from the foreground or background of their mind.

Obviously, we can all see the upside in these three noble motivations. Most likely, you resonated with some or all of them. Yet as noble as these life goals are, by themselves, they're still aiming low.

Holy Goals

Some people get up, and the thing that most occupies their thinking is, *How can I please God the most today?* These people are sensitive about making sure they do everything a follower of Jesus should do. But their holy behavior is often driven by a fear of losing something they can't possibly lose (God's love) or gaining something they already have (God's love). Their lives look pious to outsiders looking in and spiritually well ordered when you're on the inside looking out. They're conscientious about praying, reading their Bible, meditating, and keeping themselves unstained from the sinful world around them. These are very serious and devoted followers of God.

Some people get up, and the thing that most occupies their thinking is, *How can I do things today that add to my eternal reward?* These people understand that heaven is not some abstract concept but a real place, and they want to make sure they've invested well in what's waiting for them when they finally get there.

Regardless of some of the concerns you might have with these two goals, especially based on the way I framed them, we can all agree that there's some spiritual merit for those who want to please God or to make sure they're doing the kinds of things God rewards in eternity. But even these priorities can still cause us to feel we're coming up short. And I've known people who are absolutely committed to priorities like these who have marriages none of us would want.

Wealth, beauty, power, fame, family, humanity, some noble cause, pleasing God, and rewards are just a handful of examples of the kinds of things people could live their lives for. Throw in leisure, drinking, and beauty competitions, and you've got an even dozen. These priorities form the backdrop of many couples' lives and are the defining feature of their focus. In the process, they create an effect—sometimes, a catalytic one. There may be a reaction because the husband has a headlock on one while the wife is having tea with another. But even if just one priority held the collective focus of your marriage, you can see how it may have little, if anything, to do with the depth of intimacy and heart connection we enjoy. It may even work against them.

Your marriage is going to have a focus. I suggest that none of these things make sense as the primary focus of our life individually, or our focus as a couple. They may be highly leveraged B priorities, but we need to be extremely careful not to let them own first place in our heart. Here's why . . .

Drum Roll, Please

Only one thing should *own* our hearts. That *thing* is a person. His name is Jesus.

When Jesus owns our hearts, everything else and everyone else that is important to us are better off. They're safer. God's love protects them *through* us as well as *from* us. When the One who loved us first and best is the one we love first and best, everyone else in the group photo will find their stock value going up.

Darcy and I had been married about a decade when she—out of nowhere—just tasered me. She didn't use one of those real ones like the police carry, though I'm sure it's crossed her mind a few times in the years since our wedding. No, she picked up an emotional Taser gun, aimed it at my heart, and pulled the trigger.

The kids were still quite little. Diapers, dust, and dirty dishes made up the bulk of her days. More than anything else, the pervasive attitude in our relationship at that time was fatigue. Life had assigned us a piece of music with no rest signs in its score. I wouldn't say our love was lacking, but our energy, enthusiasm, and patience were running on fumes.

I decided to take the initiative and arrange a nice evening at an upscale restaurant for the two of us. Her birthday was in close enough range that I thought I could slip in a birthday gift—you know, make it a surprise. I'd gotten her a new wristwatch, had wrapped it myself, and had gone by the restaurant to arrange with the maître d' to bring it out on a dish just before they served dessert. I'd slipped a card in an envelope to go with it. Okay, here's the part I'm reluctant to mention. You're going to laugh your . . . well, you're going to think I'm a complete idiot.

I wanted to take her to a place where there was live music and somebody who sang classic love ballads. At the time, Scottsdale, Arizona, didn't offer a lot of options. In fact, on that night it only offered one: Robert Goulet. All right now, just be quiet! I was trying to do something special. I didn't have options. Michael Bublé was only about five, and Adele wasn't yet old enough to figure out which loser she'd use for the subject of her next song. I thought this would be nice: a quaint, upscale restaurant; a jazz band; and a balladeer.[1]

As we were driving there, I said, "Did you hear Robert Goulet's in town?" Darcy said, "Robert Goulet? Man, I can't stand his voice." *Uh-oh.* "Too bad our parents aren't in town," she joked. "We could have gotten them tickets."

Things started going downhill right out of the blocks. I explained to Darcy that I had no idea she had such strong opinions about him and realized that I should have done a bit more research before I planned our nice evening with her being serenaded by Mr. Goulet. Regardless, the evening was off to a bad start.

But the food was good. I told her to imagine it was Paul McCartney singing beautiful songs to her. She rolled her eyes. Then we ordered dessert, and right on cue, my maître d' buddy brought the gift and card out on a saucer. She opened the card first. But after the look it created on her face, it was irrelevant whether she opened the gift. I had written what I had thought was a poetic statement (not original to me) on the card.

Darcy,

You're my reason for living.

Love, Tim

With Goulet's rich baritone in the background and his jazz ensemble backing him with romantic chords, I watched Darcy read my note. But it didn't bring a smile to her mouth or tenderness to her eyes. She looked at it with an expression of concern. Then she put it back in the envelope and started to open her gift.

"Hold it," I said. "Did I say something wrong?" Frankly, I'm so ADHD that I had forgotten what I'd written.

She was quiet. She obviously didn't want to hurt me, but she didn't want to stay silent on what she felt we needed to keep clear between us. Finally she took out the card, placed it in front of me on the table, and said, "Tim, I don't want to be your reason for living. I *can't* be your reason for living. I don't want that kind of pressure, because I guarantee you that I will let you down. I'm human. I could never live up to the expectations of someone who needed me to be their reason for living. Plus, I'm going to die someday, and then what?"

At that moment, our romantic evening took a complete face-plant. I was hurt but also confused by the sudden diversion of the evening from romantic to philosophical. Darcy made sure I understood she wasn't talking philosophically; this was pure theology. There is only one person who can live up to the pressure and expectations of being our reason for living. It's the person who proved his qualification for that role by dying on the cross for us.

While I was trying to figure out whether to move into a defensive debate or simply write the entire evening off as a bust, here came Mr. Goulet himself, microphone in hand, telling everyone about the lovely girl sitting across from me who was celebrating her birthday. The maître d' had tipped him off. That same maître d' brought a chair up for Mr. G to sit in as he sang Darcy a tender love song. She sat there and took it in charming stride, while the rest of the restaurant crowd looked on. Some of the other women (much older women, I have to admit) were dabbing their eyes with their napkins, and when his song was over, everyone gave Mr. G and Darcy a standing ovation.

I wanted to crawl under the rug.

True Greatness

The world we live in pushes us to live great lives. That sounds like a good idea . . . unless you happen to meet Jesus along the way. Then you realize that the world's advice is a trap for fools. God's Word encourages us to live truly great lives. What's the difference? A great life is about me. But as you'll see, a *truly* great life is lived for God's glory and for the benefit of others.

Jesus said, "'Love the Lord your God with all your heart and with all your soul and with all your strength and with all your mind'; and, 'Love your neighbor as yourself'" (Luke 10:27). The best way to grasp what Jesus is conveying here is to see our love delivered at two levels. There's our primary love and then our secondary love. Our primary love has a singular focus; our secondary love has many objects, which we in turn prioritize in a descending order. When Jesus explains that our love for God should be with *all* of our heart, soul, mind, and strength, he's acknowledging that it can't be *all* if we're sharing that love with anyone else. Plus, the words he uses—*heart, soul, mind,* and *strength*—cover the totality of our whole being when we love someone. Jesus is making it clear that he wants our love for God to be our first-in-line love—a no-one-in-a-close-second-position type of commitment.

But Jesus adds something to his statement. He adds it because, technically, they're inseparable. He says, "And love your neighbor as yourself." We could see these as two different commands, and to a certain extent they are. But more accurately, they're a couplet command. Doing the first one assumes you are doing the second.

When we love God, that love can come from two sources. It can come from our human limitations, or it can be love we first received from him and are now merely giving back. The main way we know whether the love we're giving to him is from the love he first gave to us is simple: Do we have a passionate love and concern for others—in this case, our spouse? That's what a love sourced from God looks like. We can give him all of the lip service we want, but the true evidence that heavenly love is recycling through our heart is how we treat each other.

First John 4:19–21 makes this point: "We love because he first loved us. Whoever claims to love God yet hates a brother or sister is a liar. For whoever does not love their brother or sister, whom they have seen, cannot love God, whom they have not seen. And he has given us this command: Anyone who loves God must also love their brother and sister."

Keep in mind, here, that "brother" refers to anyone God calls us to love. I know couples who would prefer some wiggle room on this. They say they love God—even work overtime to serve him at their churches—but loathe their spouses. They assume they get a bye on 1 John 4:19–21 because they're so loyal to God, and their spouse is such a jerk. The Bible doesn't agree. Love that comes from God is unique: it isn't offered based on the merits of the one receiving it. Also, it's delivered in abundant quantities (more than a person needs) and graciously (as though it's an honor on the part of the giver).

Jesus set the standard for what love for a spouse should look like. His example demonstrates that true love subordinates its own position and needs for the sake of meeting the needs of our spouse. So how are you doing in that regard? You reply, "Not as well as I'd like," or worse, "Not even in the area code." Listen, you might be carrying a D-average on loving your spouse above yourself, but God's grace wants to help you ace the final.

If we took all of the scriptures we've looked at over the past few pages and synthesized them into a definition of true greatness, I think it would sound something like this:

True greatness is a passionate love for Jesus Christ that shows itself in an unquenchable love and concern for others.

This is what the Bible teaches should be the overarching goal of our lives. That's why we've made it the top floor and roof of the house drawn on the napkin earlier in the book. True greatness is the top of the heap of our priorities pointing toward the source of the grace we want to live our life by. But every part of that house has a direct application to our role as a spouse.[2] That's why we've taken its individual pieces and connected them directly to our marriage relationship. With that in mind, let's tailor this definition to the subject at hand:

True marital greatness is a passionate love for Jesus Christ that shows itself in an unquenchable love and concern for each other.

God has something he's dying to give us that will drive us to love our spouse the way he loves us.

Compelled by Grace

There's a passage of Scripture that blows me away every time I read it. It's a passage you need to dog-ear in your Bible or copy onto the notepad on your phone so you can keep it handy. It's packed with all the spiritual nutrients we need for whatever life chooses to dish up. Like a biblical lozenge you keep in the back of your marriage, spreading its soothing warmth over the sore spots of your love, this passage is a solid prescription for whatever ails you. Read this passage, and then we'll pull two prescriptions for a truly great marriage out of it:

Christ's love compels us, because we are convinced that one died for all, and therefore all died. And he died for all, that those who live should no longer live for themselves but for him who died for them and was raised again.

So from now on we regard no one from a worldly point of view. Though we once regarded Christ in this way, we do so no longer. Therefore, if anyone is in Christ, the new creation has come: The old has gone, the new is here! All this is from God, who reconciled us to himself through Christ and gave us the ministry of reconciliation: that God was reconciling the world to himself in Christ, not counting people's sins against them. And he has committed to us the message of reconciliation. (2 Corinthians 5:14–19)

I want to draw two points from this passage, each building on the other, that summarize the point of this book you're holding in your hand.

God's Love for *Us* Must Be the Driving Force in Our Life

We are not driven by *our* love for God but by *his* love for us. God's love for us is the only thing that can carry us through all that life throws at us, as well as keep all of our other priorities in balance—especially our marriage. Our love for him, though well intended, is still drawn from a bank account with credit limits. That's why the love we must give to our spouse is the love God pours over us each second of our life.

God's love, as we shall see, is an extension of his amazing grace. This love/grace has a *compelling* nature to it—meaning, among other things, we can't truly receive it and not also want to send it back outwards toward others. That's because God's grace transforms. It reboots. It does not leave us the same way it found us.

The idea behind the word translated "compels" refers to a pressure—not a pressure to control someone but a pressure that releases power to love someone. The apostle Paul is saying that God's grace compels us to love. Keep in mind, too, that Paul wrote this letter to a church known for their arrogance, pettiness, territorialism, and dysfunction. This group of believers struggled with the standard issues that couples typically bring to their marriage. But God's grace obliges those who have received it to lavish it on the people they're called to love, regardless of how unlovable they may be.

Therefore, no matter what any of us may say is the driving force of our personal lives or our marriage (wealth, beauty, power, fame, etc.), God says, "I want *my love* for you to be the driving force of your life. Anything else simply isn't going to cut it—not humanitarianism, noble causes, performing to gain my favor, earning heavenly rewards, or winning beauty contests! Please, just relax in the reality that I love you regardless of how well you jump through hoops or achieve this world's most envied trophies!"

God's Love Is Seen and Experienced in the Cross

The epitome of God's love was expressed at the cross, where he reconciled us to himself. Reconciliation—or the restoration of a relationship between enemies—compels us by God's grace to love our spouse through the power of the love God showed us at the cross. Because he reconciled us to himself, he wants us to carry on the ministry of reconciliation to others—especially our spouse. When we slip under the covers of our marriage, he's saying, "I want you to love your spouse with the love I love you with, and if there's enmity between you, I want you to let my love compel you to restore your relationship."

When the love we bring to God is drawn from the pool of our human limitations, our response to caring for our spouse comes off as anemic:

- *Oh, okay, I guess I'll drop this.*
- *Oh, okay, I guess I'll change my attitude.*
- *Oh, okay, I guess I'll be more cooperative about meeting their sexual needs.*
- *Oh, okay, I guess I'll forgive.*

No! Jesus passionately met our needs. He wants his love pouring through us to passionately meet our spouse's needs. Coming full circle, then, when we get up every morning, something is framing the bigger picture of what we're hoping to accomplish.

When a grace-filled spouse gets up, the priority that most occupies their thinking is, *How can I let God's love for me empower me to love others, especially my spouse, today?* Grace-filled people are overwhelmed with the love God poured out for them on the cross. Because they are no longer his enemy, they want to be ambassadors of his transforming grace to the people he's called them to love—starting with their spouse. They do this because they are compelled by grace.

With this in first position, we move on into our day to care for our spouse, as well as love the people we encounter as we make a living, lead, offer humanitarian aid, carry the banner for our cause, or participate in our pageants.

The Qualities of True Marital Greatness

A grace-filled marriage exudes a passionate love *from* Jesus and *for* Jesus that shows itself in an unquenchable love and concern for our spouse. This is what true marital greatness looks like. And there are four qualities of true marital greatness that are direct extensions of God's gracious heart. These four building materials complete our napkin strategy for a grace-filled marriage.

A Humble Heart

I don't know who said it first, but the best definition I've heard for *humility* is not thinking less of yourself; it's thinking of yourself less. "Do nothing out of selfish ambition or vain conceit. Rather, in humility value others above yourselves, not looking to your own interests but each of you to the interests of the others" (Philippians 2:3–4).

A Grateful Heart

This is an appreciation for what you have and for who has given it to you (both God and your spouse). "Give thanks in all circumstances; for this is God's will for you in Christ Jesus" (1 Thessalonians 5:18).

A Generous Heart

This is a great delight in sharing with your spouse all that God has entrusted to you. "Give, and it will be given to you. A good measure, pressed down, shaken together and running over, will be poured into your lap. For with the measure you use, it will be measured to you" (Luke 6:38).

A Servant's Heart

This is an attitude describing the sacrificial assistance you enthusiastically make available to meet your spouse's needs and best interests, regardless of the cost. "Whoever wants to become great among you must be your servant, and whoever wants to be first must be your slave—just as the Son of Man did not come to be served, but to serve, and to give his life as a ransom for many" (Matthew 20:26–28).

Humility, gratefulness, generosity, and a servant's heart are qualities that define a grace-filled marriage. That's how God operates in his relationship with us. You may say, "Nice try, but you haven't met my spouse. I'm married to someone who is arrogant, unappreciative, stingy, and indifferent to my needs." Well, your spouse may or may not be that way. But the fact is, we have those same kinds of attitudes toward God, and yet he continues to maintain these four gracious qualities toward us.

There are four things we can do to incline our spouse to embrace the qualities of God's grace. First, we need to decide that we will offer these four qualities as gracious gifts to our spouse, regardless of whether they *extend* them back. We do this because that's how God offers them to us—without strings attached.

Second, we need to make humility, gratefulness, generosity, and a servant's heart the *expectation* in our attitude, not the *exception*. We need to go to the "settings" section of our heart and check these four qualities as the default attitudes in how we deal with our spouse.

Third, we need to ask God for opportunities to *experience* these attitudes so that they become second nature to us. Usually, daily married life affords us ample opportunities to show our spouse humility, gratefulness, generosity, and a servant's heart.

Fourth, we need to *encourage* these qualities in our spouse by valuing and applauding them when we see them exercised. Maybe not every time. Maybe not overboard. But the Scriptures say that when we get to heaven, Jesus wants to say to us, "Well done, good and faithful servant!" (Matthew 25:23).

If God sees reason to applaud our efforts, we ought to do the same for our spouse. You might be surprised to find that your affirmation is just the thing that inclines your spouse to embrace these truly great qualities.

When True Greatness Radiates

Just think of what the qualities of humility, gratefulness, generosity, and a servant's heart could do for some of the touchier issues in your marriage. We all have times when we're beyond our wits' end. It might be about our money, body, parents, kids, stepkids, time, hobbies, personal burdens, and sex life.

Apply an attitude of humility, gratefulness, generosity, and a servant's heart to the way you handle your money, your attitude toward your spouse's body, the way you deal with each other's parents, the way you treat the kids (yours, mine, and ours), the way you handle your time, the attitude you take toward each other's hobbies, the tenderness you bring toward each other's personal burdens, and the commitment you bring toward meeting each other's sexual needs—humble sex, grateful sex, generous sex, servant-hearted sex. In all these areas, regardless of how bleak they may have been or how hopeless they presently appear—these four qualities of God's grace will help you make sure each of these categories has a green arrow pointing up!

At the Risk of Sounding Strident

We're almost done with our journey of filling our marriage with grace, nearing that point where nearing that point of summarizing our discussion and putting a period to this story. By now, you've probably discovered the overarching angle of this book. I'm coming at this whole marriage thing differently from most authors. Rather than focusing on the relationship between spouses, I'm focused on each spouse's relationship with the Creator of marriage. It goes back to my opening premise that the bigger problem in our marriage is not a lack of love but the absence of grace. Grace can't be artificially manufactured. We can muster up "nice." But *grace* comes only when we're transformed by it through a relationship with the only true source of grace, Jesus Christ.

With this in mind, there's something I've been wanting to share since I started writing this book. I want you to embrace God's grace like never before in your marriage. I want you to know his mercy when life's burdens wipe the smile off your face. But I don't think this can be done simply by reading a book like this. I think it can sure help frame the big picture for you. But a grace-filled marriage isn't an isolated decision you make—it's a commitment based on a relationship you maintain . . . with Christ.

A relationship with Christ can be no more maintained with a single decision than a relationship with our spouse can be maintained simply by stating a vow. Those kinds of things declare our good intentions, but then we have to put into that relationship a daily, sweaty, sometimes tear-filled effort.

What I want to say next could easily be misunderstood. The legalism police will be ready to scream, "Citizen's arrest!" But I'm going to take that risk.

Things That Help Grace Flourish

It's extremely difficult to maintain an attitude of grace toward our spouses without regular coaching in grace from God through his Word. God speaks to our heart through the Bible. The more we let him do that, the more his grace becomes the rule rather than the exception in our life. I'm not saying how, where, when, or how long. I'm just saying there's a cause-effect relationship between how much time we commit to strengthening our relationship with God through his Word and how much ease we enjoy when it comes to extending grace in our marriage.

It's extremely difficult to maintain an attitude of grace toward our spouse without regularly praying for our spouse. Not the kind of prayers that badger God to knock them in the head and get them to see our way of thinking, but prayers of thankfulness for their love, their efforts on our behalf, their skills and gifts, their body, their hopes, their dreams, and their joys. And we need to offer daily prayers that entreat God to help our spouse with their fears, their frustrations, their disappointments, and areas where sin is trying to get a grip on them.

I think it's also extremely difficult to maintain an attitude of grace toward our spouse if we're trying to do it in isolation, with just us two. God has placed his Spirit in many people who could be in our circle of friends. He's also put some mature grace mentors within the congregation of a local church. Grace-filled marriages are much easier to maintain when we have good friends and a good church to pick us up, hold us up, or cheer us on. Obviously, not all faith communities are grace-filled faith communities. I want to encourage you to keep looking until you find one. But once you do, pour your hearts into these people and let them love you back.

Darcy and I have been married for more than forty years now. And over those four decades, we've seen just about all you can see. Like so many couples on the front side of their journey, we were running on our own steam. Because of that, we ran out of steam quickly. We had to deal with short fuses and long grudges. It took a while for us to surrender our hearts to these commonsense priorities of a heart connection to Jesus.

It's like our discussion about our marital marathons. A decision to run a marathon is one thing, but the decision to finish one requires a daily commitment to maintain the disciplines and denials necessary to prepare for the challenge before us and to keep padding forward through its monumental demands. This is all I'm talking about here. I'm not saying that reading your Bible, praying, and going to church are going to give you a grace-filled marriage. Everything hinges on your willingness to let God's love for you flow through your heart to your spouse's heart. However, I am saying that it's hard to imagine any of us ever enjoying a grace-filled marriage without a regular connection to God through his Word, prayer, and his church.

Grace-Filled Love for Life

When we started out, our premise was pretty basic—maybe the missing ingredient in our marriage isn't love but grace. We agreed that there are wonderful passages of Scripture about marriage. But for these passages to be lived out, they assume the presence and power of God's grace. We put forth a simple observation: God is dealing with his bride, the church, in a context of grace. What if we followed suit? Why don't we treat our spouse the way God treats his?

We learned about three toxic lenses that are often chosen by one spouse to frame their attitude toward the other: the Me Lens, the Love If Lens, and the Pious Lens. We had to admit that rather than choosing which toxic lens to view our spouse through, it's much more convenient to carry all three . . . just in case. But then we suggested a fourth lens—the Grace Lens—a perspective framed by the heart of God.

Then we learned how God's grace looks, feels, and acts in the playrooms, workrooms, and bedrooms of our love. We offered a plan written out on a napkin that introduced us to a house built by God's grace—a house with four floors. The ground floor helped us learn the power God's grace has when we allow it to direct our words and actions to meet our spouse's inner needs for a secure love, a significant purpose, and a strong hope.

On the second floor, we threw open the windows and let God's fresh air of freedom waft through our love. We learned that grace-filled husbands and wives give each other the freedom to be different, vulnerable, candid, and to make mistakes.

The third floor of our grace house was the gym where we were encouraged to isolate six character muscles and work them well every day: the muscles of faith, integrity, poise, discipline, endurance, and courage.

As we climbed up to the top floor, the roof level allowed us to look over the horizon. We all have longings and leanings. It's easy to let these hog the center stage of our life, but God has a better idea. It would have been easy to assume that the punch line of this book would be that if we want to have a grace-filled marriage, we need to put our spouse first. But to the contrary, we learned that would guarantee the downfall of our marriage. To enjoy a grace-filled marriage, we need to let Christ's *love for us* be the driving force behind the love we give to our spouse. It's what people committed to having truly great marriages do. That passionate love we have for God because of what he did for us on the cross shows up in our marriage as an unquenchable love and concern for our spouse. This grace is tempered by four truly great qualities: a humble heart, a grateful heart, a generous heart, and a servant's heart.

If this were to become the default mode of our marriage, we couldn't help but enjoy a deeper, richer, and more meaningful love as couples. This could mark the end of our story, but there's more to all of this than simply what is in it for us. Sometimes, the bigger role of our grace-filled marriages is how they impact the marriages of our children.

A Daughter, a Wedding, and a Blessing

When you're whisking away to your honeymoon, the last thing on your mind is that time, many years down the road, when you'll be standing outside a reception watching your own child drive off to her honeymoon. Because of that, it behooves us all to pay attention.

Darcy and I raised four children. Our oldest, Karis, was the first one to get married. "Karis," as you may know, is the English spelling of the Greek word that is translated "grace." Being named grace doesn't guarantee her a grace-filled marriage, but we hoped that getting to watch God work through her badly-in-need-of-grace parents might have given her at least a bit of a head start. As the plans were made and the big day got closer, Karis pulled me aside and asked if I would be willing to share a blessing over her during the ceremony. Of course I agreed.

But what to say? Based on the inspiration I got from a man I admire, John Piper, I decided to share my heart's desire for my daughter in poetic form.[3] I spent an evening in my study poring over words I thought might frame this bigger message of grace, as well as serve as a poetic send off for my daughter. The last two lines are not mine. They're the closing line of one of John Piper's poems to his daughter when she got married. But what leads up to those last two lines are *this father's* attempt to speak a gracious blessing over his daughter. More than anything else, I wanted Karis to know that the success of her role as a wife was going to stand or fall not on how much she loved this man she was marrying but on how much she loved God. With this in mind, let me close this chapter with the poem I wrote for her.

A Wedding Poem for Karis

A good man stands beside you and he longs to trust your heart.
He's been loyal to his brother and a fine son from the start.
He's everything you prayed for and he puts my fears at rest,
But somewhere past this moment, life will put you to a test.

You see, it almost seems too easy in this shrine to vows and rings,
To think that you will always want to love and do good things.
But I've learned life has imposters, who can slip in through the seams,
Of a love that gets distracted by the lure of earthly themes.

And so, please let these father words sink somewhere deep inside,
And pray they hold you vigilant should life toy with your pride.
For somewhere in the future, who knows just when or where,
These fickle friends will call your bluff, and test how much you care.

Suppose you find the gifts you've honed and polished through the years,
Become a source of marvel and looked up to by your peers.
Regardless of the headlines or the stars beside your name,
Please keep your arms around this man and love him more than fame.

And should your life be blessed with far more goods than you can count,
Like Midas with his golden touch, success' silver fount.
You may be so inclined to put your heart in money's health.
Don't do it, my sweet daughter, love this man more than wealth.

You might just find that through the years your home becomes a place,
That turns each soul that visits you into a well-known face.
A home filled with contagious joy that causes hearts to blend,
In all that fun, don't fail to love this man far more than friends.

And sometimes in the clutter and the hurry of the day,
The worst might get the best of you and make you want to say,
That you're tired of all the pressures; you're weary of love's tests.
Just keep your hand clenched tight in his and love him more than rest.

And what if by divine design you're called to some great cause,
Some noble goal or effort that can haunt with fear or pause,
And should it all require a peek into the throat of death,
Just hold this man with all you've got and love him more than breath.

Oh please, dear daughter, love this man, yet do not think this odd,
Be careful that no matter what, you love him less than God.
For in the shadow of the cross, in spite of second place,
He'll know, he'll see, his heart's secure by the peace on your sweet face.

The greatest gift you give as wife is loving Christ above your life,
And so I bid you now to bless, go love him more and love him less.[4]

—

From Good to Grace

———

If you've come this far, thanks. I hope the journey has been worth the effort. You want something more from your marriage, you want to bring something better to your role as a couple, and you want to make something greater of your love story. Consider this moment a standing ovation on your behalf from Darcy and me.

There's a reason that conscientious people read books about marriage. Marriage has a way about it. There's a best-of-times, worst-of-times feel to the relationship that follows a couple from their wedding day through their life together. It's a holy tension that goes with trying to make a team out of two people who seem similar going in but who are often quite different. Then there's life. If it comes at you the way it tends to come at most people wearing wedding bands, it's easy to feel outgunned and outflanked—especially when you see how much the forces of evil keep their laser dot pointed at your heart. Add to that the drama each of you brings through your missteps, and it's not uncommon to wonder what all the celebrating was about at your wedding reception.

Our hope for you is that the best of times far outnumber the worst. Whether they have or haven't, one thing is certain: if love is all you're depending on in your marriage, you're going to run out of ideas and resolve sooner and more often than you'd prefer. That's why God offers you something more—his grace.

In these closing words to you, I don't need to add any more to our discussion on the role of God's grace in marriage. All the pages to the left of this one have worked to make that point. What I want to do is simply remind you of something you most likely know but can easily forget in the ins, outs, ups, and downs of your relationship as a couple.

There's a lot resting on your marriage. Big stuff. God's kingdom stuff. Even though you record your marriage in years, there's an eternal dimension to what your union represents to God's grander redemptive story. There are a lot of people whose lives will be impacted by how you live out your love—even people in generations way on down the line from you. Because of this, I want to encourage you by drawing your attention to something I keep on my desk.

It's a brass benchmark. This particular one is a replica of the one the US Geological Survey folks placed at the top of El Diente Peak. It's in the southwestern part of Colorado in the San Miguel Mountains. If you want to see the actual one, you'll have to climb to the 14,165 foot mark to get to where it's imbedded in rock at the apex of that summit.

I keep this replica on my desk as a reminder to me of the part marriage plays in the bigger story of time. This benchmark illustrates the strategic role of marriage in two ways: by the brass it's made of, and by the ultimate purpose it serves.[1]

Brass is an alloy of two primary metals—copper and zinc—that are very different from each other. But when they go through the extreme heat required to break them down individually so that they can meld together into a new and different property, brass, they also become something as an alloy that they could never be as individual metals.

Brass has malleable qualities. As such, it can be more easily re-formed and cast into something different than its two basic components ever could as separate entities.

Brass has great acoustic properties. There's a ring to it. That's why bells are made out of brass rather than copper or zinc (which have no ring to them individually). And just think of how much beautiful music is dependent on all of those different instruments made out of brass. In fact, an entire section of a typical orchestra is called the "brass" section. And the percussion section is also crowded with cymbals and noise makers made out of this amazing alloy.

Brass has a high tolerance for friction. That's why it's used for the gears, bearings, and tumblers in doorknobs and locks. In other words, it's the preferred metal for offering opportunities, creating safe havens, and protecting the things we hold dear.

Brass is antimicrobial. Therefore, it's germicidal. Toxic pathogens cannot thrive on its surface. Because of this, it's used in hospital rooms and operating rooms for its ability to diminish the spread of infectious microorganisms.

Brass is weather-resistant and corrosion-resistant. It can move from intense highs to punishing lows in temperature without being damaged. All these wonderful and powerful features happen only after copper and zinc are brought to a melting point through extreme heat. This allows for the process of dross removal—skimming off the contaminants and imperfections that would undermine the quality of the final alloy. This alloying process requires that the copper and zinc be melted and kept in a liquid state until they hit 2,300 degrees Fahrenheit.

Colorado has fifty-four official mountains over fourteen thousand feet. Why do you think the US Geological Survey people ask the foundry that makes their benchmarks to give so much attention to the refining process that makes the brass plate they place at the top of these peaks? Of course, they know what happens on a mountain fourteen thousand feet up. The wind, rain, sleet, blowing sand, and temperature differences are enormous. Plus, when people summit those mountains, where do you think they'll want to stand for their pictures? Exactly, right on top of the benchmark.

God has chosen marriage as his highest example to the world of his creation. He places it at the apex of civilization—the summit of humanity's story—for a reason. He wanted something that could weather the extreme demands of reckless culture and endure the radical attacks of the forces of evil. He wanted something the next generation could stand on when it came time for them to get their wedding pictures. He chose marriage. Marriage was his first thought when he made man, and it will mark the final celebration of humankind's journey when we finally join the Lord Jesus for the grand marriage reception with Jesus in heaven.

Happily ever after would be a lousy ending for the story of your marriage. It's devoid of all the challenges and refinements God meant for you to experience—things that would keep you close to him and pull you closer to each other. He needs the two of you to be a benchmark for his glory. He wants to use your marriage to mark the high point of his love in the midst of a rugged and rocky human drama. And so he takes you as individuals and, through often extreme circumstances, melts the brittleness of your heart and skims the dross from your soul, so that he can make you as a member of this marriage something you could never be for him on your own. But it's sometimes painful and, almost every time, demanding. Yet it's what it takes to meld two individuals into a beautiful and useful story of one couple. A couple who . . .

- can shine like gold but is far more durable,
- is more capable of being molded and shaped into his image,
- brings a beautiful ring to the peals of God's love story and lovely tones to his symphony of salvation,
- creates greater opportunities and higher levels of security to those who reside within the rooms of your heart,
- offers strong resistance to the diseases of sin and temptation—not just for yourselves, but for the children God gives you to raise, and
- has a higher capacity to endure the fierce weather patterns of life and resist the corrosive nature of culture.

Your refining story won't happen without setbacks—sometimes agonizing ones. And most likely, it will take longer than you'd prefer. But if you keep inviting God to add his grace to the process, ultimately your marriage will become a story . . . of him.

From good to grace—a narrative of God taking two people on an adventure through a life that ultimately leads to eternity. If you live long enough, that shiny patina gets a gray tinge to it. It's part of your story too. Gray may seem dim to others, but if God's been slipping his grace into the process of refining your lives and your love over the years, that gray ultimately shines brighter than gold. It's a time when the kids' laughter may echo in the back rooms, but they've been long since gone. It's a period when you notice sunsets more, a season of closing chapters, good-byes, and last times.

You start your love story with dreams; you end it with memories. But if you have invited Jesus along for the ride and let his grace seep its way into all those memories, you'll get to finish your story well. You'll know, indeed, that the promise of the Bible is true: his grace is sufficient. And his grace will prove to be sufficient all the way to the end of your love story . . . when one of you gently lays the other into the arms of God.

———

STUDY GUIDE

———

WELCOME TO
GRACE-FILLED MARRIAGE!

Grace
Filled Marriage
VIDEO STUDY

Take your marriage to the next level with
the Grace Filled Marriage Video Study

Love is what gets us married – but grace is
what keeps our love from growing weary,
stale, bruised, and even bitter.

Grace makes a good marriage better.
It rescues our marriage when it's in trouble.

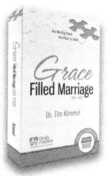

STUDY GUIDE

It's time to turn grace from a subject of a book to the substance of your relationship. For some of you, this is going to be a lot of fun! But for all of you, this has the power to transform your relationship into an amazing love story. You're going to get a chance to talk about what you've learned from the *Grace-Filled Marriage* and make it your own. We all know it's one thing to read about grace but it's an entirely different thing to actually live it out. That's what we're going to start to do right now.

Whether you're doing this study in a group, with your spouse, or on your own, below are a few suggestions to make this discussion time a safe and productive endeavor.

- **Leave your defenses** at the door. Be open and willing to learn about yourself as you listen to God's Word, to the conversation, and especially to what your spouse has to say.
- **Speak truth in love.** Anger, hurt, and frustration are all powerful feelings that are appropriate to talk about, process, and defuse, but this is not the place for them. If these have a hold on your marriage, ask your group leader or the pastoral staff at church for information about individuals who can help work you through them.
- **Share the time** with other members of the group. After all, an opportunity to speak is an opportunity to be listened to, feel respected, and see that people care about you. We can all benefit from both giving and receiving.
- **Keep all that is said confidential.** What people share in the group is never to be shared with anyone else.
- **Pray** for the group time. Ask God to guide the conversation and pour out his wisdom. Ask the Holy Spirit to do his transforming work in the hearts of those who gather.

- **Expect** God to bless the time you invest and the effort you make to fill your marriage with grace.
- **Put grace to work:** Take seriously these invitations to live out what you're reading about. Filling your marriage with grace calls for action!

PART 1: WHAT'S GRACE GOT TO DO WITH IT?

Chapter 1. The Missing Piece in Your Marriage

WARMING UP: What is the biggest thing that jumped out at you in this chapter (a point, a story, a scripture, etc.)? What do you think about that in regards to marriage in general or your marriage in particular?

Most marriages don't struggle from a lack of love; they struggle from a lack of grace (3).

1. Had you ever thought about this distinction before? Why might focusing on grace be helpful to your marriage?

When we drove away from our wedding reception, Darcy didn't realize she was riding next to a man who likes to go down dead-end roads just to make sure they truly lead nowhere. She was holding the hand of a man whose dreams consistently eclipsed his abilities to make those dreams come true. While we're checking off the full-disclosure box, I need to let you know she also married a man who struggled with seeing the little things of life—like his car keys, wallet, and wristwatch (5).

2. What are a few things your spouse didn't know about you when you got married? This might be a good time for a reality check because no one *has* the perfect spouse, and no one *is* the perfect spouse. Remember that every item mentioned is an opportunity for grace.

Grace is desiring the best for your spouse, even when they may not deserve it. . . . To have a marriage that thrives, you need grace (5).

3. What is it about our nature that makes it so hard for us to give grace to our spouse? What keeps us from loving our spouse with grace the way God loves us, his spouse? What can we do to come to a point where we struggle less?

Every married couple will have a tough time making it without grace. That's because, at the bottom line, our marriage is too much about us, individually (8).

4. In what ways is your marriage too much about *you*? If you're not sure, realize that identifying areas of disappointment can help you answer that question.

Satisfaction [in marriage] only comes when we have grace to adjust to all of the ins and outs of change that life brings our way (9).

5. What changes have most challenged your marriage? How have you weathered them?

6. What have you learned to help you weather the next changes better?

REAL-LIFE GRACE: What do you find most challenging, enlightening, or encouraging as you consider filling your marriage with more grace? Let this guide you in creating a personal goal for this week. *My Personal Goal:*

Chapter 2. *Weaving Grace into Your Love Story*

WARMING UP: What is the biggest thing that jumped out at you in this chapter (a point, a story, a scripture, etc.)? What do you think about that in regards to marriage in general or your marriage in particular?

When you look at a woman's braided hair, it appears that two strands of hair are overlapping each other from the top to the bottom. It looks like two . . . but I was holding three in my hand. As I thought of that friend we have in Jesus— and Darcy and me trying to figure out life, parenting, and love together—it hit me that . . . a grace-filled marriage is more about weaving together three people than it is joining together a man and a woman (16).

1. How are you doing at establishing God as the foundation, the heart, the life source, and the glue of your relationship? What especially has worked well?

When you and your spouse got married, God's design was to braid your love and hopes and dreams for each other together with his. He wanted to slip among the two of you and weave his grace into your love story (17).

2. Reflect on your marriage and talk about the evidence you see of God braiding your love, hopes, and dreams for each other into his.

To have a grace-filled marriage, first we need to recognize the graceless ways we tend to view our spouse. Then we will learn how to replace those distorted views with a grace-filled perspective (18).

3. Think about your initial reaction to the story of Mia, Rick, and Rick's dad (18–20). Whose side were you on? Did that allegiance change? Why or why not?

4. The Me Lens: What could you do to turn the focus away from you and communicate an "I believe in you" type of love to your spouse? What could your spouse do/say to help you harness your potential and bring out your best?

5. The Love If Lens: Share with your spouse one or two examples of when you feel as if the love being offered you is conditional.

6. The Pious Lens: Confess where you might be self-righteous in your relationship. In what ways, if any, are you using your knowledge of the Bible to control your spouse with spiritual guilt and shame?

Rick and Mia . . . picked up a different lens: clean, clear, and with a divine focus. This lens's perspective was all about the best interests of the one being viewed through it rather than the one holding it. It was the Grace Lens. They got it directly from the nail-scarred hand of God's only begotten Son (31).

7. Maybe it was a teacher, a coach, a church worker, a grandparent, an aunt, or an uncle. Who in your life has looked at you through the Grace Lens? What impact did that person's perspective have on you?

REAL-LIFE GRACE: This week, how will you more readily choose the Grace Lens as you look at your spouse and/or ensure that God's presence is the third strand of your marriage braid? *My Personal Goal:*

Chapter 3. *A Grace-Filled Perspective*

WARMING UP: What is the biggest thing that jumped out at you in this chapter (a point, a story, a scripture, etc.)? What do you think about that in regards to marriage in general or your marriage in particular?

Regardless of how much relational capital a couple has going into their marriage, if they keep a balance sheet on each other's behavior, the addition of one person's downside will subtract from the other person's level of commitment, multiply their frustrations with each other, and ultimately divide their hearts (35).

1. Whether it was the nest egg that vanished, the pink slip that came, the misstep, the tours to Iraq and Afghanistan, or something else, you may have found yourself involved in this kind of math. What are some of the reasons we maintain this kind of marital balance sheet?

2. What can we do to combat this tendency and these reasons you just identified? The list on page 36 offers some helpful suggestions to get you started.

3. Have you ever before viewed Jesus' sacrifice on the cross as a personal marriage proposal to you? How does that impact you?

Our marriage can't come close to what it could be until we accept Christ's work as it truly is, on his gracious terms. Until then, we'll always struggle to extend grace to our spouse. It's hard to give what we struggle to receive (37).

4. Why would the authors consider God's amazing grace *the defining factor of your relationship with your spouse*? Do you agree? Why or why not?

5. Have you struggled with "credit card focus" on certain issues? How would an attitude of God's grace deal with that kind of focus?

Grace isn't blind. Nor is it without nerve endings. A call to a grace-filled marriage doesn't mean we ignore, trivialize, or excuse our spouse's unacceptable behavior. Grace doesn't mean we lose our voice when it comes to dealing head-on with things that are clearly out of line. And grace doesn't remove consequences. God's grace is offered to us, but it isn't realized if we're unwilling to receive it properly. We have to repent. And our repentance must be more than an "Oh, excuse me, Lord. I'm sorry." It requires us to own our actions and refuse to continue in our self-destructive ways (46).

6. Why do we fail to address our own or our spouse's unacceptable behavior?

7. What are some tips for successfully speaking the truth in love? How should we respond when grace must be tough?

Grace is not our default mode. It's contrary to our hardwiring. But there are two things we need to know. First, the Holy Spirit can give us the power to flip off the switch of our self-protective default mode regardless of how bad the circumstances get in our marriage. Second, although there's pain in choosing to exercise grace, there's far more pain, sorrow, and fallout when we choose not to (47).

8. Review the story of Phil and Jan. What most impressed you about the way they handled the consequences of the affair? Who benefitted from their choices?

REAL-LIFE GRACE: *Your relationship to each other will stand or fall primarily on your relationship with Christ. . . . So love God first and love God most (55).* Keeping in mind this crucial truth, look at the houses drawn on pages 54 and 55. Based on your knowledge of your spouse and your awareness of your own weaknesses, write out this week's goal (potentially fourfold). What will you start doing today to help your spouse *aim at true greatness, build character, experience four freedoms,* and satisfy their *three inner needs?* My Personal Goals:

PART 2: WHAT DOES GRACE LOOK LIKE IN A MARRIAGE?

Chapter 4. *Grace Gives You a Secure Love*

WARMING UP: What is the biggest thing that jumped out at you in this chapter (a point, a story, a scripture, etc.)? What do you think about that in regards to marriage in general or your marriage in particular?

We are called to raise our spouse's sense of security by loving them in a way that causes them to grow more confident about how dearly they are loved by us. A secure love makes it much easier to give and receive grace. So Darcy and

I came up with a definition of love that has proven to thrive under fire: Love is the commitment of my will to your needs and best interests, regardless of the cost *(65)*.

1. Brag on your spouse! Share a time when meeting your need for a secure love had a pretty high price tag.

2. Sometimes what's in our spouse's best interests is tough and gritty love. Think about a time when your spouse or a friend has loved you this way. What have you come to appreciate about that bold act of meeting your need for a secure love?

We feel insecure when our spouse refuses to accept the things about us that are simply us. I'm not talking about weaknesses that can stand improvement. Nor am I talking about bad habits or unacceptable behavior. I'm talking about the things about us that aren't right or wrong but just are. They're our personality quirks, mannerisms, physical abilities, and body types . . . to name a few. They're the things that make each of us one of a kind (66).

3. What aspect of who you are drives your spouse a little (or a lot) crazy?

4. What are a few of the things that make your spouse one of a kind that you struggle to accept?

5. What can we do to become more accepting of each other? And what can we do to bring out the best in our spouse and thereby strengthen their sense of security?

One of the ways you value your spouse is by being interested in the things that interest them. You notice. You care. Honor is also about empathy. When you honor your spouse, you value your spouse so much that you can't contain the "woo-hoos!" on their behalf in victory, and you likewise hurt deeply with them in defeat (71).

6. Which of your spouse's interests or passions would you be wise to accept more completely and genuinely?

7. What would that acceptance look like (actions) and sound like (words)?

8. Which of your own interests and passions do you wish your spouse would choose to accept more readily? What actions and words would communicate to you that new acceptance?

Our sexual relationship is the litmus test of how serious we are about being an agent of God's grace when it comes to our spouse. . . . A married person should see meeting their spouse's sexual needs as one of their primary ministries to that person (74, 81).

9. Explain in your own words the connection between sex and grace. How should grace impact our tendencies toward the wrong attitudes toward sex in the section entitled "The Antithesis of Grace-Filled Sex"?

10. Why is it helpful to think of meeting the sexual needs of one's spouse as ministry to that person?

A man's need for sexual fulfillment with his wife is more than just a physical need. It is comparable to our need as women to feel loved and accepted. What if we needed to spend time with our husband, desperately longed for some attention from him, or hadn't heard him tell us he loved us for a while . . . ? How would we feel if he said he was too busy, too tired, or not in the mood to respond to these needs? . . . For most of our husbands, there is no greater way for them to feel love and acceptance from us than sexual fulfillment. This is a need God has put in them that he asks us to fulfill to the best of our ability (81).

11. After reading Darcy's statement, what did you find surprising? Helpful? Reassuring?

12. What are your thoughts about having a "convenience-store attitude" toward each other's need and desire for sex? Do you feel your thoughts align with God's grace? How would this impact each spouse's battles with sexual temptation (their internal red lights or green lights)?

REAL-LIFE GRACE: Your sexual relationship with your spouse reveals how serious you are about being an agent of God's grace to them. At some point in this coming week, what specific step will you take to *accept* your spouse; demonstrate an interest in your spouse's interests (*affiliation*); give meaningful touch more frequently and lavishly; and/or offer your mate grace-filled sex (*affection*)? *My Personal Goals:*

Chapter 5. *Grace Gives You a Significant Purpose*

WARMING UP: What is the biggest thing that jumped out at you in this chapter (a point, a story, a scripture, etc.)? What do you think about that in regards to marriage in general or your marriage in particular?

The grace to help your spouse sense a significant purpose will draw your hearts closer.... Even in those times when there's nothing to be happy about, a grace-filled commitment to meet each other's need for significance enables us to navigate our way through life's downturns (87).

1. Why is meeting "each other's need for significance" a worthwhile topic to address during premarital counseling? What immediate or ongoing impact could building up your spouse's sense of significance have on a marriage?

When the Me Lens, Love If Lens, or Pious Lens slips between us and our spouse, it's next to impossible to meet their need to feel significant. The Grace Lens, however, sees beyond their shortcomings to their intrinsic value. That's because with God's grace-filled perspective, we're empowered to notice the contribution our spouse is making and the potential they have yet to realize—you know, the same way God sees us (90).

2. Just as we want to love our spouse in a way that makes them feel loved, we want to encourage our spouse in ways that make them feel significant. So be specific. Next time you are discouraged, what would you like your spouse to do to encourage you? (If you don't know, how can your spouse know?)

I'd like you to meet Dan and Ann. They're really good-looking. They told me . . . There's nothing wrong with a couple being taken with each other physically. That's fairly normal. But for Dan and Ann, physical appearance was all they focused on. I hoped that they would expand their attraction to each other beyond the depth of each other's skin (96).

3. How much pressure do your feel from culture or the way you were raised to put too much of your emphasis on superficial features (like looks, resume, or pedigree)? How could/should God's grace impact that perspective?

What I mean by significance *is a healthy view of who you are and what you have to offer as a person created by God and paid for by his Son on the cross. . . . God didn't create us by accident or empower us at random. He made us to make a difference. When we do, we not only fulfill his purposes but push glory toward him in the process. And we compound our capacity for significance even more when we turn "making a difference" into a byline of our marriage relationship (93).*

4. Which of the verses that you read in this chapter—Psalm 139:14, Ephesians 2:10, Philippians 2:13, Micah 6:8, Luke 6:27–31—do you find especially empowering as you consider your God-given purpose? Explain what you understand your significant purpose to be.

The more you sense you're contributing to the big picture of life, the more significant you feel. The more significant you feel, the more at peace you are with yourself, your spouse, and God. The more at peace you are, the more you enjoy your life and your marriage (95).

5. Think about whether the current dynamic between you and your spouse is pointing your significance fuel meter toward full or empty. The best way to turn your spouse into someone who makes you feel more significant is to dedicate yourself to making your spouse feel more significant. What can you be doing toward that end?

6. Brainstorm ways that a marriage can fill both spouses' inner need for significance in each of these categories: general influence, specific roles, relational touch, and spiritual impact (97–101).

*Our spouse feels a significant purpose when we **affirm** them . . . But this goes beyond just noticing what a spouse does (which is very important). Affirmation also voices appreciation for what a spouse is. . . . Our spouse feels a significant purpose when we give them our **attention**. Grace-filled couples give each other access to their schedules and first right of refusal to major shifts in plans. But it's much more than that. A spouse feels valuable when we notice what they notice, when we care about what they care about, when we know what they're up against and maneuver our time, resources, and focus to be there for them when they need us. . . . Our spouse feels a significant purpose when we give them **admonition** . . . You admonish your spouse by speaking up when their actions or attitudes need a course correction. And you build their sense of value by respecting their areas of strength so much that you're open to their critique. . . . (98, 102, 103, 105, 107).*

7. In the Bible study meltdown by the MLB pitcher's wife, who did you relate more to? How does grace impact your opinion?

8. Which is hardest for you to extend to your spouse—affirmation, attention, or admonition? Why do you think that is—and what will you do to get better at it?

REAL-LIFE GRACE: Husbands, figure out two or three ways to let your wife know this week she is more to you than lover, mother, and date-night companion. Wives, in two or three different ways this week, let your husband know he is far more to you than provider, protector, and sperm donor. *My Personal Goals:*

Chapter 6. *Grace Gives You a Strong Hope*

WARMING UP: What is the biggest thing that jumped out at you in this chapter (a point, a story, a scripture, etc.)? What do you think about that in regards to marriage in general or your marriage in particular?

God is in the hope business. . . . He wants to give us the strength to face the everyday challenges that come our way, as well as a hope to carry us through circumstances that are bigger than any person is equipped to face. . . . Grace-filled marriages recognize this need for a strong hope and help spouses with holes in this area to see beyond their fears (113–14).

1. What waves are currently breaking around you and your spouse? What can you do—individually and together—to keep your eyes on Jesus and keep walking toward him?

When people spend a lot of time focusing on the things they fear, they have a hard time looking optimistically at the present, let alone the future. And they shouldn't be surprised that they lack confidence in God's ability to sustain them and protect them. . . .God wants us to operate in an attitude of faith that shows itself in an ongoing ease at trusting him (116, 118).

2. What effect does—or could—the unshakable truth of God's sovereignty have on your level of fear? Explain. How might that affect the level of hope you experience in your life and marriage?

3. Think about control issues you may have. In what fears, if any, might they be rooted? Find Scripture that speaks against this fear and consider memorizing it.

I can tell when a couple's sense of inner strength is high or low simply by how at ease they make me feel when I'm around them. Are their hearts open or guarded? Do they see a change of plans as a crisis or simply as a change of plans? Do they view an unknown primarily as a risk or an opportunity? When they talk about their struggles in general, do they voice words of confidence or intimidation? Do they convey a sense of vigor or weakness about the challenges in their life? Do they sound as if they're taking their cues from the Word of God or from the latest cable news update? Marital love can only blossom and grow when it envisions a hopeful future (118).

4. Where do you resonate most in this paragraph: the examples of fear or the examples of trust?

5. Why does hope help love blossom, and why can a lack of hope cause love to wither?

6. What will you and your spouse do to nourish hope? What can you do to diminish fear about real dangers and sadness over real setbacks?

There are specific grace-filled exercises we can add to our marriage that empower us to use our words and actions to help build a strong hope into our mate. . . . Our spouse feels a strong hope when we encourage their God-given **abilities**. *. . . Our spouse feels a strong hope when we encourage them toward great* **accomplishments** *(121, 123).*

7. Kit and Wayne were greater than the sum of their parts as Kit led Neighborhood Ministries and Wayne played his critical role of cheering for her. What God-given abilities have you seen in your spouse and/or what has your spouse seen in you that led to others' benefit and God's glory?

8. Reflect on the Teacher of the Year story (123–24). In what ways has your spouse mentored you, encouraged you, and believed in you?

9. In what ways could you encourage your spouse to fulfill a long-held dream? If you're not sure, ask.

One of the best ways to build a strong hope is to live a mighty spiritual **adventure**. . . . *Adventures require taking risks, facing unknowns, and processing fear. Last time I checked, risks, unknowns, and fear are things God loves to lead us through. You can't live a life of genuine faith without being willing to follow God into places you'd prefer to avoid—trusting him all the way (125–26).*

10. When have you and your spouse chosen safety over strength? What might have resulted in the situation, in each of you, and in your marriage if you had stepped out in faith?

11. When have you and your spouse chosen strength over safety? What did you learn from the experience, whether it was a victory or a defeat?

REAL-LIFE GRACE: Describe a current set of circumstances that gives you the opportunity to choose between safety and strength. Consider the pros and cons of your options; think through what is keeping you from trusting God and choosing adventure. *My Personal Goal:*

Chapter 7. Grace Frees You to Be Different and Vulnerable

WARMING UP: What is the biggest thing that jumped out at you in this chapter (a point, a story, a scripture, etc.)? What do you think about that in regards to marriage in general or your marriage in particular?

The primary source of our secure love, significant purpose, and strong hope is Jesus. . . . Jesus went to a lot of trouble to set our hearts free. He didn't die on the cross to free us to be able to do whatever we want. He freed us to be able to do what he created us to do without artificially imposed restraints.

This is a huge point when it comes to marriage. The grace that saved us is the grace that's supposed to show up in marriage with unfettered love and uncluttered devotion. Jesus wants us to show each other a love that doesn't make wrongs out of nothings, doesn't trivialize our spouse's feelings, doesn't stifle their concerns, and doesn't withhold mercy when they've lost their way and are trying to get back (129, 131–32).

1. Jesus freed us to do what he created us to do. How do your purpose and your spouse's purpose interact and complement one other?

2. What is limiting love in your marriage? What is cluttering your devotion to your spouse? How will you respond?

Earlier, we were introduced to a napkin strategy for a grace-filled marriage. It was a house with four levels. In the past three chapters, we looked at the first level listed on that house diagram—meeting our spouse's three driving inner needs [the need for a secure love, a significant purpose, and a strong hope]. In this chapter and the next, we will unpack that second level of the house and look at four freedoms we can give our spouse as agents of God's grace (132).

The freedom to be different: *We tend to see what we like about the person we're falling in love with rather than what annoys us. Add to this the reality that we are continually morphing to adjust to what life brings us along our journey, and you can see why it's vital that grace-filled spouses give each other the freedom to be different (132–33).*

3. Think back to your dating days. What did you do back then to woo each other that you've stopped doing now?

4. Grace chooses to celebrate the quirks a spouse either has or develops and to make those quirks part of the love story. What turkey-calling quirks in your spouse do you need to embrace with grace? Or, metaphorically speaking, what are the dirty-socks areas in your marriage where you need to "Get over it, accept it, celebrate it, and protect it!"

The freedom to be vulnerable: *Grace-filled marriages recognize that there are things that knock a spouse off their game, things that need to be treated with tenderness, understanding, and patience—things like monthly cycles, pink slips, moving, rebellious children, and bad health reports. We need to create an atmosphere within our marriage where our spouse doesn't feel they have to wear a mask around us to keep from revealing where they are emotionally. They need to know that the deeper hurt or confusion within their heart can come out without fear of being attacked (141).*

5. What keeps you from being transparent and vulnerable with your spouse?

6. What keeps you from being accepting and gentle when your spouse is transparent and vulnerable with you?

7. And when it's your turn to be different and vulnerable, what expression of grace means the most to you? Make sure your spouse knows what you need and want.

REAL-LIFE GRACE: Consider writing your spouse a love letter. It doesn't need to be long or fancy, clever or flowery. It simply needs to be authentic and from the heart. In this letter consider sharing your innermost feelings about the things you value in your spouse and how he or she makes you feel (not just physical characteristics or traits you like). *My Personal Goal:*

Chapter 8. *Grace Frees You to Be Candid and Make Mistakes*

WARMING UP: What is the biggest thing that jumped out at you in this chapter (a point, a story, a scripture, etc.)? What do you think about that in regards to marriage in general or your marriage in particular?

There are two aspects of marriage that tend to generate the most angst in our hearts: how we communicate our deep feelings to each other, and how we process the foolish choices we make individually—choices that often score a direct hit to the heart of our spouse (147).

The freedom to be candid: *Communication is vital to a marriage relationship. . . . A deeply loving relationship between a husband and wife needs to encourage a free exchange of the feelings churning within their hearts. A grace-filled spouse wants to communicate clearly and deeply with their mate, but not pummel their heart in the process (150).*

1. Remember the references to sledgehammers, thumbtacks, and Jerry Springer? What are some things that keep us from drenching our honesty in grace rather than using a sledgehammer to make a point? What can we do about those things that trip us up?

2. Think about a time when someone spoke a difficult truth to you with gracious candor. What did you notice and appreciate about that approach? What did you learn about how to speak candidly to someone you care about?

In a grace-filled marriage, spouses know they can vocalize their deep troubles or concerns graciously, and they are equally committed when they are the recipient to take the words to heart (157).

3. Darcy shared how the context of her family of origin complicated her ability to both be candid and respond gracefully to Tim's candor. Can you relate?

4. Revisit the valuable lesson that *the goal of the discussion should always be unity, never victory.* Why is this wise? Why is this a goal of grace?

The freedom to make mistakes: *This last dimension of grace is the hardest freedom for most people of faith to grant to their spouse. The reason it's so tough is because in marriage, we're no longer two but one. Our mistakes, whether past or present, affect both of us. Therefore, when our spouse really messes up, usually we have to pay a high personal price for their folly (161).*

5. What was your takeaway from Chad and Tracy's story (162–67)?

6. Why is their punitive reaction to each other's mistakes even worse than the mistakes themselves?

7. Following Jesus' example of double vision can keep us from walking down that punitive path Chad and Tracy chose. Describe that double vision and reflect on its grace and wisdom.

We are more inclined to condemn when we've lost sight of the enormous forgiveness we've received from God. But we can rise above this in a grace-filled marriage. Darcy and I have found that our relationship is better when we preach the gospel to ourselves individually every day—when we remember the undeserved grace God has given us. It's much easier to look past the pointed edges of our spouse's sin—even with its personal cost to us—when we focus on their desperate need for rescue (170).

8. What hope-filled and encouraging truth(s) can you take away from the conclusion to Chad and Tracy's story (171–72)?

9. Repenting of one's sin is very different from being sorry about having to deal with its consequences. *True repentance doesn't minimize the severity of crimes, make excuses, or pass the buck. It stands up,*

speaks up, owns up, and then shuts up. It assumes there are conse-quences for actions and willingly steps forward to take its lumps (172). Why is true repentance an essential starting point for rebuilding a marriage?

REAL-LIFE GRACE: Grace thrives when we meet our spouse's need for a se-cure love, a significant purpose, and a strong hope, as well as when we give our spouse the freedom to be different, vulnerable, candid, and to make mistakes. These only happen when we operate in the power of God's grace. As you reflect on these counterintuitive truths, what do you see about yourself, and what do you feel nudged to do to strengthen your marriage? *My Personal Goals:*

Chapter 9. *The Character of Grace*

WARMING UP: What is the biggest thing that jumped out at you in this chapter (a point, a story, a scripture, etc.)? What do you think about that in regards to marriage in general or your marriage in particular?

If anything's a marathon, marriage sure is. . . . God has [glorious things] for all of us on our marriage marathons. That is, if we do what needs to be done to prepare ourselves for the race and then manage ourselves wisely along the way (176).

1. Think about the different aspects of a marathon and of preparing for one. Why is a marathon an especially apt metaphor for marriage?

The third level of our grace-filled napkin strategy addresses the character that sustains our commitment to meeting each other's inner needs, maintaining a climate of grace, and living for something bigger and more important than ourselves (179).

2. Six character muscles are key to finishing strong in a marriage: faith, integrity, poise, disciplines, endurance, and courage. *Over the years I've noticed that when a couple has trouble, it is always because one or both spouses have chosen not to exercise one or more of these character muscles (182).* Which of those six muscles of yours are in good shape? Would your spouse agree? Which one is in the most need of exercise in your life?

The Character Muscle of Faith: *Hebrews 11:6 [reads,] "Without faith it is impossible to please God, because anyone who comes to him must believe that he exists and that he rewards those who earnestly seek him" (183).*

3. Look again at the five questions listed on page 184. What did your initial answers—before you read the answers directed by the truth of God's Word—reveal to you about your level of faith in God, both individually and as a couple? Is there a pressing situation in your life today you need to approach in faith?

The Character Muscle of Integrity: *We live in a world that is extremely tough on people who choose to do the right thing. . . . Yet when we choose integrity, it's another way that the love God showed for us on the cross is given back to him in obedience (188–189).*

4. When has your commitment to being a person of integrity cost you? When has it paid off? When has not being a person of integrity resulted in something you regret?

The Character Muscle of Poise: *When we travel close to God's heart, he keeps us from getting out of balance. . . . Regarding this poise muscle group that helps us maintain moral, spiritual, relational, physical, emotional, social, theological, and intellectual equilibrium, King Solomon said, "Whoever fears God will avoid all extremes" (Ecclesiastes 7:18). . . . If you'd like a working definition of poise to give you direction, try this:* **poise is a keen spiritual sense of what is appropriate** *(191–193).*

5. Are you or your spouse better at exercising this poise muscle group—whether moral, spiritual, relational, physical, emotional, social, theological, or intellectual equilibrium. Share some examples of how poise was the key factor in past successes.

6. Share an example of how the more poised spouse strengthens the poise of the other.

The Character Muscle of Discipline: *The best way to understand the power behind discipline is to look at its synonyms: self-control, order, obedience, restraint, and confinement. . . . A great analogy would be the rails of a train. . . . As long as the train stays on those tracks, it exercises enormous power. But should it ever leave those tracks, it is forever known by a different name: a train wreck. . . . Spiritually disciplined couples do three things: they delay gratification because of* advance *decision making* in order to stay on target toward *a focused goal (196–97).*

7. Reflect on past experiences where discipline has led to you and your spouse achieving a shared goal.

8. Discuss which area your spouse is more disciplined in than you. If you two are radically different, what do you do to avoid annoying one other? Is this an area that needs improvement?

The Character Muscle of Endurance: *We must be serious about continuing all the way to the end because of all the things we encounter along the way that incline us to quit. . . . God's Spirit empowers us as his grace keeps us padding forward through the good, the bad, and the revolting sections of the course before us (198).*

9. Talk about some of the rough patches, the curveballs, the dark seasons of life that you have had to endure? How has your spouse's inner strength been an encouragement to you?

10. Maybe there isn't a significant difference between how the two of you deal with tough times. If that's the case, describe how the two of you help—or could better help—each other when life is hard.

The Character Muscle of Courage: *God knows we're going to face things that frighten us, but he promises to give us all we need to overcome. Over the years, Darcy and I have learned that the only thing we need to face any fear is a greater fear. . . . We've learned that there is one fear that helps us rise above all others—the fear of God (201).*

11. Define *fear of God*. Think through why this fear of God helps us rise above all other fears we may encounter. Can you see a relationship between fearing God and realizing more of his grace? Give an example.

12. In what ways has your marriage been like the couple who got married before the NYC Marathon and finished together in a heap? What part of their story do you need to adopt into your story?

REAL-LIFE GRACE: We can choose a marriage that exudes a contagious faith, consistent integrity, practical poise, personal discipline, steadfast endurance, and inspirational courage. To have these, we've got to go to God's gym on a regular basis (202). Take a minute to be your own personal trainer. Outline a week of workouts in God's gym. When will you pray? Read God's Word? Worship? Gather with his people? Spend some time alone with him? Sometimes you and your spouse could work out together. At the end of the week, consider fine-tuning the workout schedule for the following week. *My Personal Goals:*

Chapter 10. The Heart Qualities of Grace

WARMING UP: What is the biggest thing that jumped out at you in this chapter (a point, a story, a scripture, etc.)? What do you think about that in regards to marriage in general or your marriage in particular?

Every married couple's relationship is defined by something. That something will determine the color, flavor, texture, melody, and scent of the love in our marriage. . . . Every marriage is aimed somewhere even if that somewhere is nowhere. Since it's not a case of if we're aiming our marriage, but where, why not aim it at something bigger than ourselves (206–7)?

1. Wealth, beauty, power, and fame are often the dreams that guide people's lives. Explain how dreams of wealth, beauty, power, and fame may in fact be God-given gifts and actually his calling on a person's life. Reflect on how these dreams can also creep into our lives in detrimental ways, and whether they're at work in your life now in in ways that could be toxic to your ultimate love story.

2. Why can the pursuit of any one of these goals cause a couple to miss the depth and passion of intimate love?

3. Think about your list of life priorities and where the goals of serving family, helping the poor, and making the world a better place fall on that list. What reordering of your goals might God be calling you to do?

Wealth, beauty, power, fame, family, humanity, some noble cause, pleasing God, and rewards are just a handful of examples of the kinds of things people could live their lives for. Throw in leisure, drinking, and beauty competitions, and you've got an even dozen. . . .

Your marriage is going to have a focus . . . [but] none of these things make sense as the primary focus of our life individually, or our focus as a couple. They may be highly leveraged B priorities, but we need to be extremely careful not to let them own first place in our heart (211).

4. What percentage of your heart does Jesus own? Why did you choose that number? What dynamics are competing for the same real estate?

5. In what ways do you see your spouse loving God and loving others with their whole being? Be encouraged when it's your turn to listen to your spouse's answers to these two questions.

Jesus set the standard for what love for a spouse should look like. His example demonstrates that true love subordinates its own position and needs for the sake of meeting the needs of our spouse. . . .

True marital greatness is a passionate love for Jesus Christ that shows itself in an unquenchable love and concern for each other (217–18).

6. Affirm your spouse for a recent example of Christlike love. You might even ask your spouse for a recent situation when you could have shown them love that was more Christlike and grace-filled.

7. Can you relate to Darcy's reaction to her having to be a person's "reason for living"? Explain in your words the difference between loving your spouse with your power as compared to loving your spouse through the power of Christ's love for you (2 Corinthians 5:14–19). How are you doing on that?

When a grace-filled spouse gets up, the priority that most occupies their thinking is, How can I let God's love for me empower me to love others, especially my spouse, today? *. . . A grace-filled marriage exudes a passionate love from Jesus and for Jesus that shows itself in an unquenchable love and concern for our spouse (221–22).*

8. A **humble heart** (thinking of yourself less); a **grateful heart** (an appreciation for what you have and for God who gave it all to you); a **generous heart** (sharing with your spouse all God has entrusted to you); a **servant's heart** (*the sacrificial assistance you enthusiastically make available to meet your spouse's needs and best interests, regardless of the cost [223]*)—which of these qualities comes most easily to you? Which presents the greatest struggle? What steps can you take toward humility, gratitude, generosity, and a willingness to serve?

9. Tim advised his daughter to love her spouse more than fame, wealth, friends, rest, and her very life. But he exhorted her to make sure that no matter what, she always loved her spouse less than God. How would putting your love for God above your spouse change your ability to maintain a grace-filled marriage?

REAL-LIFE GRACE: Review the section "Grace-Filled Love for Life" that starts on page 227. What are you and your spouse doing—or will you do—in each of these areas to develop and strengthen your attitude and increase your acts of grace? How does the advice about the study of the Word, prayer, maintaining fellowship with a gracious community of believers, and having a softhearted willingness to love your spouse with the Lord's love play into your ultimate plan for enjoying grace-filled love for life? *My Personal Goals:*

NOTES

CHAPTER 1: The Missing Piece in Your Marriage

1. If you'd like an excellent biblical and theological conversation about these passages, I highly recommend Tim Keller (with his wife, Kathy's, input), *The Meaning of Marriage: Facing the Complexities of Commitment with Wisdom from God* (New York: Dutton, 2011), and John Piper (with his wife, Noël's, input), *This Momentary Marriage* (Wheaton, IL: Crossway, 2009).

2. God's overarching grace is a point that both Keller and Piper passionately drive home as they deal with these standard passages.

3. Examples we've seen of spouses misusing biblical principles of marriage include wives browbeating husbands for not being the "spiritual leader" of the family, husbands insisting on micromanaging their wife and telling her she's required to submit—even to things that go against clear moral teaching in the Bible—one spouse insisting on isolation from the other spouse's parents under the guise of obeying the "leave" command in Genesis 2:24, a husband using a misunderstanding of "weaker partner" in 1 Peter 3:7 to keep his wife out of all financial decisions, either spouse demanding sex using 1 Corinthians 7:4, and so on.

CHAPTER 2: Weaving Grace into Your Love Story

1. If you'd like to learn how God's grace comes to the rescue in high-controlling relationships, you might want to check out Tim Kimmel, *The High Cost of High Control* (Scottsdale, AZ: Family Matters, 2005). Available at FamilyMatters.net.

2. If you know what I'm talking about here and want some extra help on dealing with your own loss of blessing, I highly recommend Gary Smalley and John Trent, *The Blessing* (Nashville: Thomas Nelson, 1990).

CHAPTER 3: A Grace-Filled Perspective

1. Depending on your age, you might or might not be familiar with this. The acronym *lol* is a short way to say "laugh out loud" as a text-message response on your mobile device.

2. If you want to go a bit higher up the learning curve when it comes to "getting grace," I encourage you to read Max Lucado, *Grace: More Than We Deserve, Greater Than We Imagine* (Nashville: Thomas Nelson, 2012), and Andy Stanley, *The Grace of God* (Nashville: Thomas Nelson, 2010).

CHAPTER 4: Grace Gives You a Secure Love

1. If you want to know how to meet these three needs in your children, you might want to check out Tim Kimmel, *Grace-Based Parenting* (Nashville: Thomas Nelson, 2004).

CHAPTER 5: Grace Gives You a Significant Purpose

1. Gene A. Getz, *The Measure of a Man*, rev. ed. (Ventura, CA: Regal, 2004).

2. Most likely, there's a Weekend to Remember event happening near you. If not, make it a getaway. You can learn all about these events at FamilyLife.com. If Darcy or I are speaking, stop by and introduce yourself. We'd love to meet you.

CHAPTER 6: Grace Gives You a Strong Hope

1. Tim Kimmel, *The High Cost of High Control* (Scottsdale, AZ: Family Matters, 2005), 13.

2. To learn more about Kit and Wayne Danley and Neighborhood Ministries, check out www.nmphx.com.

CHAPTER 10: The Heart Qualities of Grace

1. For you younger readers, Robert Goulet was a singer and actor who had enjoyed his peak as an entertainer about two decades before this incident happened.

2. If you'd like to see how that house built by grace applies to your role as a parent, see the following the three inner needs and four freedoms: *Grace-Based Parenting* (Nashville: Thomas Nelson, 2004); character: *Raising Kids Who Turn Out Right* (Scottsdale, AZ: Family Matters, 1989); true greatness: *Raising Kids for True Greatness* (Nashville: Thomas Nelson, 2006). To see how grace applies to your role as a grandparent: *Extreme Grandparenting* (Carol Stream, IL: Tyndale, 2007). To see how grace applies to your church: *Connecting Church and Home* (Nashville: Randall House, 2013). *Extreme Grandparenting* is by Tim and Darcy Kimmel. All the other books are by Tim Kimmel.

3. John Piper has written a lot of poems over the years, especially for his children.

4. Tim Kimmel, "A Wedding Poem for Karis," copyright 2001. The last two lines are borrowed with permission from "Love Him More, Love Him Less" by John Piper.

EPILOGUE: From Good to Grace

1. I want to thank a dear friend, Bob Horner, for this analogy. Bob's family owned a foundry. He grew up dealing with all kinds of metals and alloys. After he explained to me the properties of brass and how they compare to the properties a husband and wife who have allowed God to meld them into one singular, strong married couple, I bought this benchmark. Bob and Jan Horner are not only great spokespeople for strong marriages but also one of the best examples of a grace-filled marriage you'll ever find.

Other Books and Resources by Tim Kimmel

BOOKS

Little House on the Freeway
Raising Kids Who Turn Out Right
Homegrown Heroes
High Cost of High Control
Basic Training for a Few Good Men
Grace-Based Parenting
50 Ways to Really Love Your Kids
Raising Kids for True Greatness
Extreme Grandparenting
In Praise of Plan B
Connecting Church and Home

SMALL-GROUP DVD STUDIES

The Hurried Family
Grace-Based Parenting, Parts I, II, and III
Basic Training for a Few Good Men
Extreme Grandparenting
Grace Filled Marriage

TOOLS

Discover Your Child's Heart with the
Kid's Flag Page

For these and other resources for your family, go to
FamilyMatters.net

IF YOU ENJOYED THIS BOOK, WILL YOU CONSIDER SHARING THE MESSAGE WITH OTHERS?

Mention the book in a blog post or through Facebook, Twitter, Pinterest, or upload a picture through Instagram.

Recommend this book to those in your small group, book club, workplace, and classes.

Head over to facebook.com/FamilyMatters, "LIKE" the page, and post a comment as to what you enjoyed the most.

Tweet "I recommend reading #GraceFilledMarriage by @Family_Matters // @worthypub"

Pick up a copy for someone you know who would be challenged and encouraged by this message.

Write a book review online.

Visit us at worthypublishing.com

twitter.com/worthypub

worthypub.tumblr.com

facebook.com/worthypublishing

pinterest.com/worthypub

instagram.com/worthypub

youtube.com/worthypublishing